The Sig
of Four

Arthur Conan Doyle

ford
erature
mpanions

Notes and activities: Annie Fox
Series consultant: Peter Buckroyd

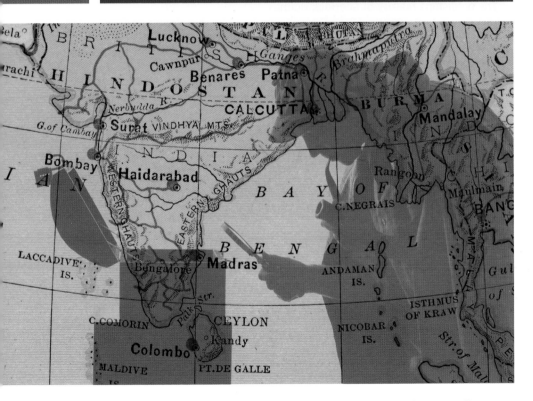

OXFORD
UNIVERSITY PRESS

Contents

What are Oxford Literature Companions?

Oxford Literature Companions is a series designed to provide you with comprehensive support for popular set texts. You can use the Companion alongside your novel, using relevant sections during your studies or using the book as a whole for revision.

Each Companion includes detailed guidance and practical activities on:

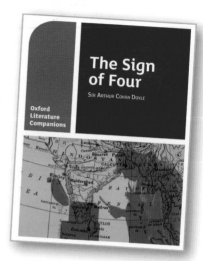

- Plot and Structure
- Context
- Characters
- Language
- Themes
- Skills and Practice

How does this book help with exam preparation?

As well as providing guidance on key areas of the play, throughout this book you will also find 'Upgrade' features. These are tips to help with your exam preparation and performance.

In addition, in the extensive **Skills and Practice** chapter, the **Exam skills** section provides detailed guidance on areas such as how to prepare for the exam, understanding the question, planning your response and hints for what to do (or not do) in the exam.

In the **Skills and Practice** chapter there is also a bank of **Sample questions** and **Sample answers**. The **Sample answers** are marked and include annotations and a summative comment.

How does this book help with terminology?

Throughout the book, key terms are highlighted in the text and explained on the same page. There is also a detailed **Glossary** at the end of the book that explains, in the context of the novel, all the relevant literary terms highlighted in this book.

How does this book work?

Each book in the Oxford Literature Companions series follows the same approach and includes the following features:

- **Key quotations** from the novel
- **Key terms** explained on the page and linked to a complete glossary at the end of the book
- **Activity boxes** to help improve your understanding of the text
- **Upgrade** tips to help prepare you for your assessment

To help illustrate the features in this book, here are two annotated pages taken from this Oxford Literature Companion:

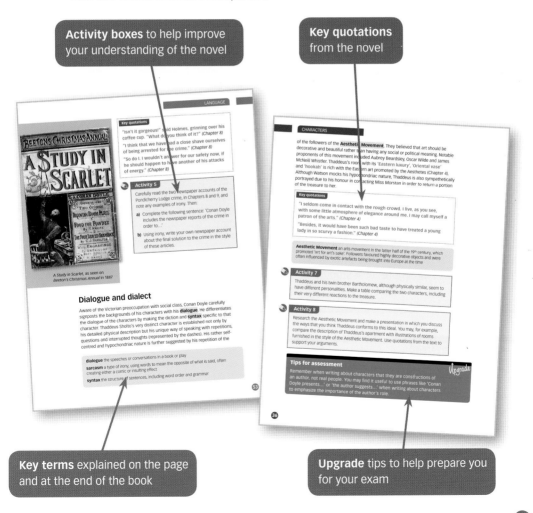

Activity boxes to help improve your understanding of the novel

Key quotations from the novel

Key terms explained on the page and at the end of the book

Upgrade tips to help prepare you for your exam

Plot and Structure

Plot

The Sign of Four, by Arthur Conan Doyle, is the second Sherlock Holmes novel. The plot follows the famous detective as he unravels the mystery of a missing father, a hidden treasure and a seemingly impossible murder. The tale is recounted by Sherlock Holmes's loyal companion, Dr Watson.

Chapter 1: The Science of Deduction

Dr Watson, the novel's **narrator**, bemoans Sherlock Holmes's tendency to indulge in **"artificial stimulants"**, in this case, cocaine. Holmes says he craves **"mental exaltation"** and is bored because he does not currently have a case for detection. He proudly explains his position as the world's only **"unofficial consulting detective"**, helping out the professionals when they are **"out of their depths"**. As a challenge, Dr Watson hands him a watch and asks him to deduce who its owner was.

Holmes correctly reads the clues in the watch and announces that it belonged to Watson's unfortunate deceased brother. The chapter ends with the announcement that a young woman has arrived and wishes to see Holmes.

Sherlock Holmes takes a scientific approach to solving crime, as shown here in a reconstruction of 'his desk', at the Oregon Museum of Science and Industry (OMSI) in the United States

- The contrasting nature of the characters of Holmes and Watson is established in the opening chapter.

- Holmes's analysis of Watson's brother's watch demonstrates both his brilliant skills of observation and deduction, but also exposes his cold nature.

- Watson's role of chronicler of Holmes's adventures is explained in the discussion of Watson's 'brochure' of *A Study in Scarlet*, which was actually the title of the first Sherlock Holmes story, published in 1887.

Key quotations

"But I abhor the dull routine of existence. I crave for mental exaltation."

"Detection is, or ought to be, an exact science, and should be treated in the same cold and unemotional manner."

"Eliminate all other factors, and the one which remains must be the truth."

"I had forgotten how personal and painful a thing it might be to you."

---

narrator a person who tells a story

Activity 1

Watson undergoes several changes of emotion in Chapter 1 from the point when he hands the watch to Holmes until he says, "I regret the injustice I did you…". Make a bullet point list of each emotion he feels, supported by a quotation from the text.

Tips for assessment

Although it is important to show that you have understood the plot of the novel, the examiner will never ask you to simply retell the story. Remember to focus on the question and how the writer conveys his ideas through various techniques.

Chapter 2: The Statement of the Case

Miss Mary Morstan, a 26-year-old governess, enters Holmes's room and explains the baffling case of her father. He had been an officer in an Indian regiment and, after her mother's death, had placed Miss Morstan in a boarding school. Ten years ago, when she was 17, he returned to England and asked her to meet him at the Langham Hotel in London, but he disappeared before they were reunited. She contacted her father's closest friend, Major Sholto, who claimed not to know that her father was in England. After answering an advertisement requesting her address, she had, for the past six years, upon the same date, received a box containing a single, rare pearl. To add to the mystery, on that morning, she received a letter saying she was a 'wronged woman', asking her to come to the Lyceum Theatre and advising her that she could bring two friends. Holmes and Watson agree to accompany her to this meeting.

- Watson finds Miss Morstan "a very attractive woman" while Holmes claims not to notice. This establishes the **theme** of romance versus science and again emphasizes the contrast between Holmes and Watson.
- The reader is introduced to many of the initial **clues** upon which this mystery will revolve.
- Watson finds himself attracted to Miss Morstan, but feels that his 'weak banking account' is an obstacle to a romance.

> **Key quotations**
>
> "You really are an **automaton** – a calculating machine," I cried. "There is something positively inhuman in you at times."
> "A client is to me a mere unit, a factor in a problem."

automaton a mechanical device that appears to be human

clue evidence used for the detection of crime

theme a topic or idea that appears in literature

Activity 2

Throughout the novel you will be provided with clues to the mystery. Keep a log book and, in no more than 100 words for each entry, record the key evidence provided in every chapter.

Chapter 3: In Quest of a Solution

Holmes has discovered that Major Sholto, the late Captain Morstan's friend, passed away six years ago. Holmes believes that Sholto's heir must know something about the mystery and perhaps is hoping to compensate Miss Morstan. They set off for the meeting at the Lyceum Theatre and Miss Morstan shows Holmes a **"curious paper"**, which she has discovered in her late father's belongings. It is a diagram with various notations, including a **"curious hieroglyphic"** of four crosses and the phrase 'The sign of the four', along with four names. At the theatre they are met by a man who ushers them into a carriage and drives them to a terraced house in the southern suburbs of London. An Asian servant answers the door and a voice from within asks that they be shown in.

- Further clues are introduced to the reader, including the words of the title, 'The sign of the four'.
- Watson continues to be impressed by Miss Morstan and her 'perfect' self-control.
- A strong sense of place is established in this chapter, with the **atmosphere** of London vividly evoked.

Key quotations

'There was, to my mind, something eerie and ghostlike in the endless process of faces which flitted across these narrow bars of light – sad faces and glad, haggard and merry.'
'Holmes alone could rise superior to petty influences.'
'We were driving to an unknown place, on an unknown errand.'

---

atmosphere the mood or tone established in the writing

hieroglyphic writing that resembles Ancient Egyptian scripts, which used pictures and symbols

Activity 3

This chapter contains the first of several key scenes that take place at night. With your partner, discuss how the mood of this chapter would have been different had it been set in the morning.

Chapter 4: The Story of the Bald-Headed Man

The bald-headed man of the chapter heading is Thaddeus Sholto, one of Major Sholto's sons. He is an eccentric character who has turned his outwardly ordinary house into a luxurious and exotic apartment. He explains that his father returned from India a very wealthy man, but he was also fearful of being attacked and frightened of men with wooden legs. On his deathbed, he confessed that he and Captain Morstan had argued over the division of treasure from India and that Morstan had died suddenly of a heart attack. Fearing that he would be accused of murder, Major Sholto and his manservant hid Captain Morstan's body and deprived Miss Morstan of her inheritance. Regretting this, Major Sholto wanted his twin sons Thaddeus and Bartholomew to make reparation but, just as he was going to reveal the location of the rest of the treasure, he was startled by a mysterious face at the window and died. Thaddeus arranged for the pearls to be sent to Miss Morstan as a small reparation, but now Bartholomew has discovered the rest of the treasure. Thaddeus has arranged for them all to travel to Pondicherry Lodge to demand Miss Morstan's share, which would make her a wealthy heiress.

- Thaddeus Sholto is introduced as a key character in the mystery and is contrasted with his twin brother Bartholomew.
- Captain Morstan's death is confirmed.
- Although outwardly happy for Miss Morstan's possible inheritance, Dr Watson sees her new wealth as an additional obstacle to a relationship with her.
- An aspect of comedy is introduced in Thaddeus's **hypochondriac** nature and Dr Watson's distracted replies.

Key quotations

'In that sorry house it looked as out of place as a diamond of the first water in a setting of brass.'

"The cursed greed which has been my besetting sin through life has withheld from her the treasure, half at least of which should have been hers. And yet I have made no use of it myself, so blind and foolish a thing is **avarice**."

"It was a bearded, hairy face, with wild cruel eyes and an expression of concentrated **malevolence**."

---

avarice extreme greed or desire for wealth

hypochondriac a person with exaggerated worries about his or her health

malevolence the state of wishing ill on others or having evil intentions

Activity 4

Conan Doyle establishes a strong sense of place throughout the novel. Carefully read the description of Thaddeus Sholto's home and then answer the following question: How do Thaddeus Sholto's surroundings reflect his character?

Chapter 5: The Tragedy of Pondicherry Lodge

Upon arriving at Pondicherry Lodge, there are signs that the grounds were dug up by Bartholomew when looking for the treasure. The housekeeper Mrs Bernstone is heard crying. She explains that Bartholomew had locked himself in his room and would not answer her. Holmes and Watson break down the door and discover that Bartholomew is dead. On the table near the dead man is a mysterious hammer-like object and a piece of paper with the sign of four on it. Stuck near the dead man's ear is something that looks like a thorn. Thaddeus notices that the treasure is missing and Holmes sends him off to report the crime to the police.

- A strong sense of atmosphere is created in the eerie description of Pondicherry Lodge.
- Watson and Miss Morstan grow closer.
- Mystery is created around how a man in a 'locked room' could have been murdered.

Key quotations

'The vast size of the building, with its gloom and its deathly silence, struck a chill to the heart.'

'A wondrous subtle thing is love, for here were we two, who had never seen each other before that day, between whom no word or even look of affection had ever passed, and yet now in an hour of trouble our hands instinctively sought each other.'

'The features were set, however, in a horrible smile, a fixed and unnatural grin, which in that still and moonlit room was more jarring to the nerves than any scowl or contortion.'

Activity 5

In Chapter 5, the reader is given a great deal of important information about Bartholomew Sholto's room. With a partner, discuss what you have learned about the crime and write down at least three questions you have about it. Then write down three quotations that show how Conan Doyle is creating an air of mystery and suspense. Discuss how this chapter may be a turning point in the novel.

Tips for assessment

When writing about the novel, you may be expected to include evidence that you have understood the plot. You should make sure that what you write is factually correct, but you should never simply retell the events of the novel. Instead, make sure you are referring to:

- recurring themes or ideas
- insight into characters and their relationships
- understanding of how the story is shaped by the author
- turning points and resolutions.

Chapter 6: Sherlock Holmes Gives a Demonstration

Holmes examines the room and discovers that two people must have committed the murder. A man with a wooden leg would have entered through the window using a rope thrown down by the second person, who entered through a hole in the roof. The footprints of the second person were unusually small, like those of a child. The dead man is thought to have been poisoned by the thorn (actually a poisoned dart) that was found in his head. Athelney Jones, a police detective, arrives. He comes to a number of false conclusions and is intent on arresting Thaddeus for the murder of his brother. Holmes says that he can clear Thaddeus and names Jonathan Small as the wooden-legged ex-convict who had been in the room the previous evening. He asks Watson to escort Miss Morstan to her home and then to bring back Toby, a dog with 'the most amazing power of scent'.

- Athelney Jones feels a sense of rivalry with Holmes and tries unsuccessfully to outwit him, adding an element of **comic relief**.
- The reader is provided with a range of clues to analyse.
- The tone of this chapter is considerably lighter and more comic than the previous chapter.

> **Key quotations**
>
> "You see that I am weaving my web round Thaddeus. The net begins to close upon him."
>
> "Then I shall study the great Jones's methods and listen to his not too delicate sarcasms."

comic relief amusing or light-hearted episodes that provide a break or contrast from more serious aspects

Activity 6

Athelney Jones is an important character introduced in this chapter. Working with a partner, locate all the key quotations that show that he feels competitive with Sherlock Holmes.

Chapter 7: The Episode of the Barrel

After returning Miss Morstan to her home, Watson borrows Toby the dog and returns to Pondicherry Lodge. The police detective, Jones, has arrested not only Thaddeus, but most other members of the household, giving Watson and Holmes the opportunity to explore the area and possible escape routes for the murderers. Toby smells the creosote that one of the murderers stepped in and they follow the dog's lead throughout the night as he chases the scent across much of south London. During this journey Holmes explains how he knew so much about Jonathan Small, who is the wooden-legged ex-convict they are pursuing, along with his mysterious companion. After some indecision, Toby leads them to a large barrel full of creosote.

- This journey, ending at dawn, allows an opportunity for **exposition** when Holmes explains to Watson (and the reader) his understanding of the case so far.
- Insights are provided into Holmes's **philosophy**.
- Although only a dog, Toby is established as a vivid character in his own right.
- The chapter ends on a comic note, as they have been led to a barrel of creosote rather than the criminals.

Key quotations

"How small we feel with our petty ambitions and strivings in the presence of the great elemental forces of Nature!"

'Toby ceased to advance but began to run backward and forward […] the very picture of canine indecision.'

exposition description and explanation of ideas; usually used in the first part of a novel when characters and themes are introduced, but also used elsewhere, for example to give background information

philosophy a set of beliefs or values that underpin the way one chooses to live one's life and understand the surrounding world

Activity 7

a) Conan Doyle uses an unusual number of place names in this chapter. Discuss with a partner how the journey is made more interesting through his listing of the locations.

b) If possible, get a map of London and the surrounding areas and trace all the locations mentioned in the novel.

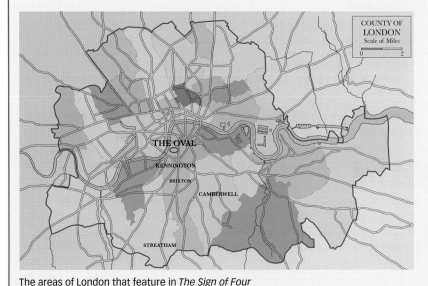

The areas of London that feature in *The Sign of Four*

Chapter 8: The Baker Street Irregulars

Retracing their steps, they once again pick up the trail of the suspects, but find it leads them to a riverside landing stage where boats are available for hire. Holmes tricks the wife of the owner of the boats to reveal that a wooden-legged man has been associating with her husband Mordecai Smith, and that they are on a steamboat called the *Aurora*. Returning to Baker Street, Holmes and Watson read a newspaper article, which praises the Police Detective Jones's **'single vigorous and masterful mind'** and his handling of the case. The Baker Street Irregulars, a noisy group of street urchins employed by Holmes, arrive and he orders them to find the *Aurora*. Holmes reveals what he knows about Jonathan Small's companion, who is an aborigine from the Andaman Islands.

- Holmes reveals his methods of interviewing to Watson.
- Holmes shows more respect for the methods of the Baker Street Irregulars than those of the conventional police force.

- The inclusion of the inaccurate newspaper article provides **irony** and could be viewed both as a criticism of journalism and of conventional police detectives like Jones.
- Watson puzzles over the **paradox** that he must devote himself to recovering Miss Morstan's fortune, which if recovered will put her out of his reach.

Key quotations

'If Holmes could work to find the criminals, I had a tenfold stronger reason to urge me on to find the treasure.'

'As he spoke, there came a swift pattering of naked feet upon the stairs, a clatter of high voices, and in rushed a dozen dirty and ragged little **street Arabs**.'

"Diminutive foot-marks, toes never fettered by boots, naked feet, stone-headed wooden mace, great agility, small poisoned darts."

Activity 8

The newspaper account is very flattering to Detective Jones. Pick out all the key phrases, such as his **'trained and experienced faculties'**, which make clear that the report is biased in his favour. Contrast these points with Watson's account of the events. Why do you think that Conan Doyle has included these two different reports of the investigation?

Chapter 9: A Break in the Chain

Watson returns Toby to his owner and goes to see Miss Morstan and her employer Mrs Forrester, relating to them the facts of the case known to him so far. Upon returning to Baker Street, the landlady Mrs Hudson tells him of her concern about Holmes's health, as he has been particularly agitated. In the morning, Holmes decides to go out to discover the *Aurora* himself. He leaves Watson as his representative at the flat. Watson sees that Holmes has placed an advertisement in the newspaper offering a reward for information to help locate Mordecai Smith and his son Jim. Athelney Jones arrives in response to a telegram from Holmes. While waiting for Holmes to return, an ancient sailor arrives, claiming to have knowledge of Mordecai Smith, which he refuses to tell anyone but Sherlock Holmes. After being persuaded to remain, the sailor removes his disguise and reveals himself to be Sherlock Holmes. He asks Jones to be **'under my orders'** when they go to arrest the culprits and says Jones will be **'welcome to all the official credit'**. Holmes insists that the three of them have dinner together.

- Mrs Forrester serves to highlight the **melodramatic** nature of the story so far.
- Jones's character is more modest and subdued than previously.
- Holmes demonstrates his remarkable ability for disguise.

- A variety of other styles of text can be noted in this chapter: an advertisement, a newspaper article and a telegram.

Key quotations

"It is a romance!" cried Mrs Forrester. "An injured lady, half a million in treasure, a black cannibal, and a wooden-legged ruffian. They take the place of the conventional dragon or wicked earl."

"This infernal problem is consuming me."

'Was it not possible that his nimble and speculative mind had built up this wild theory upon faulty premises?'

Activity 9

The meaning of the title of this chapter, 'A Break in the Chain', is not as obvious as that of most of the other chapters. Why do you think Conan Doyle gave it this title?

Chapter 10: The End of the Islander

After dinner, the three men set off in a police launch in pursuit of the *Aurora*. Holmes explains that he has realized that Mordecai Smith must have put the boat in with a repairer to hide it while the men made arrangements to escape abroad. Having located the shipyard, they follow the *Aurora* as it speeds away. They spot Jonathan Small at the stern, as well as his small companion. When Tonga raises a blowpipe to his lips, Holmes and Watson both shoot him and he falls into the river. Trying to escape, Small jumps off the boat on to the muddy banks, but his wooden leg sinks 'into the sodden soil'. He and the Smiths are captured, and Holmes and Watson locate the treasure chest. Returning to the police launch, they notice a 'murderous dart' and realize how close to death they had been.

- This is an exciting **chase sequence**, a key feature in many detective stories.
- The night-time setting adds to the excitement and mystery of the chapter.
- More of Holmes's philosophy is revealed.

chase sequence an exciting, action-packed hunt for a person or object

irony words that express the opposite of what is meant; the difference between what may be expected and what actually occurs

melodramatic having the features of a melodrama, a popular type of play in Victorian times, typically containing extreme characters, exaggerated emotions and sentimental themes

paradox an apparently contradictory statement or situation, such as Watson wanting to find the treasure and also hoping that he doesn't

street Arabs homeless children or urchins; this term, rarely used now, is sometimes seen as offensive as it refers to the nomadic life of Arabs

Key quotations

"Individuals vary, but percentages remain constant."

'... but never did sport give me such a wild thrill as this mad, flying man-hunt down the Thames.'

'I caught one glimpse of his venomous, menacing eyes amid the white swirl of the waters.'

'Somewhere in the dark ooze at the bottom of the Thames lie the bones of that strange visitor to our shores.'

Activity 10

Imagine you have been asked to film the boat chase from this chapter. Draw a storyboard with at least ten frames, showing the key moments from this sequence. Annotate it with any special effects or dialogue you would use.

Chapter 11: The Great Agra Treasure

The captured Small is given a cigar and a drink by Holmes who begins to question him. Small tells the men that the key to the treasure chest is at the bottom of the river. Watson is entrusted to bring the chest to Miss Morstan. He tells her of the adventure they have had and presents her with the treasure chest. Using a poker from the fireplace, Watson opens the chest and they discover that it is empty. Without thinking, he exclaims, **"Thank God!"** He admits that he loves her and, now that her riches are no longer an obstacle, he feels that he can declare this. She replies, **"Then I say 'Thank God', too"** and Watson draws her close to him.

- This chapter begins the **denouement** with the unravelling of the various plot elements.
- The romantic **sub-plot** between Watson and Miss Morstan is resolved.

Key quotations

'It seemed to me that there was more sorrow than anger in his rigid and contained countenance.'

'Whoever had lost a treasure, I knew that night that I had gained one.'

The treasure chest is empty

> **denouement** the final part of a novel when the various strands of the plot are brought together and resolved; also called the resolution
>
> **sub-plot** a second plot, which runs alongside the main plot

Activity 11

Suspense is an important element in mystery stories. How does Conan Doyle increase the suspense before the treasure chest is opened?

Tips for assessment

Remember when writing about the novel to use the correct literary terminology, such as 'denouement' or 'sub-plot'.

Chapter 12: The Strange Story of Jonathan Small

Small dominates this chapter, recounting the events leading up to his imprisonment, his escape and his desire for revenge. He admits that he has thrown the treasure into the Thames since, if he couldn't have it, he wanted to make sure that no one else did. He tells his story starting with his days in Worcestershire, his enlisting in the army and then being posted to India. There, through an unfortunate encounter with a crocodile, he lost his leg. After a series of adventures, he found himself guarding an entrance to a fort where two Sikh guards convinced him to take part in a robbery and murder, organized by another Sikh. These became the four in the 'sign of the four'. They hid the treasure, but were convicted of the murder.

While in prison, Small assisted a doctor and learned his skills. He also overheard the conversations of the officers and doctor when they were playing cards and discovered that Major Sholto was in financial difficulties. He proposed that if Sholto helped Small escape, Sholto and his friend Captain Morstan could have a share in the treasure. However, he was double-crossed when Sholto stole the treasure and returned to England without fulfilling any of his obligations. Small used his skills to save Tonga's life, the small aborigine who became his faithful friend, and they escaped to England together seeking revenge upon Major Sholto. Small confirms Holmes's version of Sholto's death and is taken away by Jones.

Watson confesses that he has proposed to Miss Morstan, to Holmes's distinct lack of enthusiasm. The novel ends with Holmes returning to his previous boredom and reaching for a cocaine bottle.

- Small's lengthy exposition introduces many new characters and locations.
- Small is presented with some sympathy, despite his many disreputable acts.
- The vigorous Holmes of the previous chapters is replaced by the lazy, bored Holmes of the first chapter.

Key quotations

"There we were all four tied by the leg and with precious little chance of ever getting out again, while we each held a secret which might have put each of us in a palace if we could only have made use of it."

"A fitting wind-up to an extremely interesting case."

"But love is an emotional thing, and whatever is emotional is opposed to that true cold reason which I place above all things."

Activity 12

Sherlock Holmes describes Small's tale as a "fitting wind up to an extremely interesting case". However, you may not agree. Write a speech for a debate either defending or criticizing Conan Doyle's final chapter.

Writing about plot

To prepare for writing about the plot, try the following:

- Test yourself on the order of events.
- Note how and when characters are introduced.
- Learn all the characters' names, relationships and, if appropriate, occupations.
- Connect the locations in the novel with the key events of the plot.

Structure

Structure of detective fiction

> 'What the detective story is about is not murder but the restoration of order.' (P.D. James, detective story writer)

Detective fiction must involve a crime or mystery that needs to be solved but, unlike other mysteries, the initial focus is usually on the detective. The Sherlock Holmes tales, like *The Sign of Four*, often begin with Holmes and Watson in Baker Street, with Watson offering an admiring (and sometimes exasperated) description of Holmes and his remarkable abilities, which serves as the novel's initial exposition. Next a client arrives presenting a crime or mystery that must be sufficiently interesting for Holmes (and the reader), which provides a **catalyst** for the subsequent actions. A series of puzzling clues (like the mysterious 'sign of four' notes) is presented and there must be obstacles or **complications** to prevent a quick and straightforward solution (such

Sherlock Holmes is often seen as the quintessential English detective

as a murder within a 'locked room'). An exciting **climax** is needed, which may involve chasing and trapping the criminal, followed by a full confession by the criminal, which serves as the novel's denouement.

> **catalyst** something that causes an event
>
> **climax** the most exciting and tense section of the novel, which usually occurs near the end
>
> **complication** a plot or character detail that increases interest and is not easily resolved

 Activity 13

Draw a graph like the one below. As you read the novel, chart when the tension rises and falls in the novel. After you have finished, try to locate when there are examples of exposition, complications, climaxes and denouement.

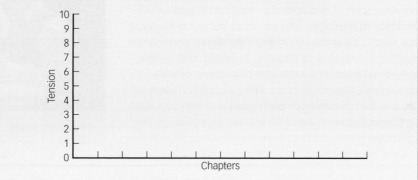

Sub-plot

Alongside the main plot of the mystery of *The Sign of Four* is the sub-plot romance between Watson and Mary. Although many fewer words are spent on this sub-plot than the mystery, it provides a vital counterpoint to the main story and reveals the differences between the characters of Watson and Holmes. In the course of the novel, Watson is immediately attracted to Mary; grows to admire her; has his hopes dashed by the prospect of her inheritance; and then, upon learning that the treasure has vanished, proposes to her. The last chapter ends with Watson's happy announcement of his impending marriage, contrasting with Holmes's slipping back into a dark depression.

Activity 13

Look at the quotations below. Then write when in the sub-plot each one occurs and what it tells us about the relationship between Watson and Mary:

Quotation	Effect on the romantic sub-plot
'I have never looked upon a face which gave a clearer promise of a refined and sensitive nature.' *(Chapter 2)*	*Watson's first impression of Mary. Start of sub-plot. Looks at her 'nature', not just her beauty.*
"What a very attractive woman!" *(Chapter 2)*	
'A wondrous subtle thing is love, for here were we two, who had never seen each other before that day… and yet now in an hour of trouble our hands instinctively sought for each other.' *(Chapter 5)*	
'Was it fair, was it honourable, that a half-pay surgeon should take such advantage of an intimacy which chance had brought about?' *(Chapter 7)*	
"Now that they are gone I can tell you how I love you." *(Chapter 11)*	
"Miss Morstan has done me the honour to accept me as a husband in prospective." *(Chapter 12)*	

Narrator

A striking feature of *The Sign of Four* and other Sherlock Holmes stories is the use of Watson as the narrator. Many novelists, such as Jane Austen in *Pride and Prejudice*, use **omniscient narrators** who are not characters in the novel, but instead are written in the **third person** by an unnamed narrator, providing an all-knowing, all-seeing point of view, able to comment on the thoughts and actions of many characters. Other novelists use **first-person narrators**, who are the main characters or **protagonists** in the novel, such as Charles Dickens's use of Pip in *Great Expectations*. This allows the reader to follow the tale completely through the point of view of the main character.

Watson, the writer

Conan Doyle employs a first-person narrator, but instead of seeing the story from Sherlock Holmes's point of view, we read the mystery from the perspective of his devoted follower, Watson. This was done to sustain the suspense in the stories, as Holmes's thoughts are not always revealed to us as they occur. If the reader arrived at solutions as quickly as the protagonist Holmes does, then the novel would lack mystery and end very abruptly. However, with Watson as our narrator, we trace the plot in the same way as a reasonably intelligent and sensible person might, but without Holmes's rapid genius. Many critics believe that Watson serves as a **proxy** for the reader and we are able to marvel at Holmes's talents in a similar way to him.

Additionally, in this age of **Realism**, Watson provides an excuse for writing the tales by explaining that he has written about previous adventures for publication. He makes clear in the narrative that he is recounting something that happened in the past while occasionally referring to the present, such as his wife reminding him of what happened on the trip from the Lyceum Theatre: **"To this day she declares that I told her one moving anecdote as to how a musket looked into my tent at the dead of night..."** This removes a degree of suspense, as it reveals both that Watson and Mary will survive this encounter and that later they will be together.

first-person narrator a narrator who is usually one of the characters in the novel and writes about events from a single perspective, using the word 'I'

omniscient narrator an all-knowing narrator who can relate the thoughts and feelings of many characters, usually written in the third person

protagonist the central character in the novel

proxy a person who represents someone else

Realism a literary movement that began in the mid-19th century and encouraged looking at the world as it really is rather than in a more romantic, implausible way. Realist authors often focused more on middle- and working-class characters and recounted the details of their everyday lives. Although Conan Doyle is not a typical realist author, aspects of this movement can be found in his work

third-person narrator the form used by omniscient narrators, which uses 'he' or 'she' rather than 'I'

Key quotations

"I was never so struck by anything in my life. I even embodied it in a small brochure, with the somewhat fantastic title, 'A Study in Scarlet'. " *(Chapter 1)*

"You have attempted to tinge it with romanticism, which produces much the same effect as if you worked a love-story or an elopement into the fifth proposition of Euclid." *(Chapter 1)*

Activity 14

Choose a short extract from the novel and try writing it in the following different narrative voices:

- in the third person as an omniscient narrator
- in the first person, from Sherlock Holmes's point of view
- in the first person, from Mrs Hudson's point of view.

What are the strengths and weaknesses of each of these choices?

Timescale

One of the appealing aspects of the story is its fast pace and this is increased by the tight timescale of events, as only four days pass from Miss Morstan's entrance to the solution of the mystery. There is also a circular nature to the story as it begins and ends with Holmes in a depressed state, reaching for a solution in cocaine.

Activity 15

Look at the table below and add any other details you believe are important. When do most of the actions take place? What do you notice about the timing of important events?

Day/Time	Events
Day 1: afternoon	Watson chides Holmes for taking cocaine. Miss Morstan visits and presents her case.
Day 1: evening/night	Holmes returns from researching Sholto. Miss Morstan, Holmes and Watson go to the Lyceum Theatre and then to Thaddeus Sholto's suburban house in south London. They arrive at Pondicherry Lodge and discover the murder. Athelney Jones arrives.
Day 2: middle of the night/early morning	Watson escorts Miss Watson back to Mrs Cecil Forrester's home. He picks up Toby the dog from a shop in Lambeth and returns to Pondicherry Lodge. Toby traces scent to the riverside.
Day 2: morning	Back at Baker Street for bath, breakfast and newspapers. Baker Street Irregulars are given orders to watch for boat. Watson finally sleeps, while Holmes plays the violin.
Day 2: late afternoon	Watson returns Toby and visits Miss Morstan.
Day 2: evening	Watson returns to Baker Street. Holmes has gone out and Mrs Hudson is worried.
Day 3: morning	Holmes returns during the night, but does not sleep. They await news of the boat. Sherlock is morose.
Day 4: morning	Holmes, dressed as a sailor, leaves. Watson monitors messages and newspapers.
Day 4: afternoon	Jones comes to Baker Street. A mysterious man arrives and reveals himself to be Holmes. A police launch is ordered.
Day 4: evening/night	A 'merry' dinner followed by a boat chase. Tonga dies. Small is captured. Watson proposes to Miss Morstan. Holmes hears Small's confession. Holmes and Watson return to Baker Street.

Flashbacks

Although most of the novel is Watson's **chronological** account of the case, there are several sections in which other characters take over the narrative by telling lengthy back stories or **flashbacks** that either further the mystery or provide explanations. Among the important flashbacks is Mary Morstan's story in Chapter 2 beginning **"Briefly... the facts are these..."**. This provides the catalyst for the investigation. In Chapter 4, Thaddeus Sholto continues the story by relaying his section of the mystery when he starts, **"I can give you every information..."** Most significantly, Jonathan Small takes over the narrative in the lengthy final chapter when he explains the mystery of the sign of four, promising that what he says **"is God's truth, every word"**. His story provides the solution to the mystery and the resolution of the novel.

Activity 16

Mary Morstan, Thaddeus Sholto and Jonathan Small all have distinctive ways of relating their stories. Write a paragraph comparing:

- their **diction** and phrasing
- what they reveal about their own personalities
- Holmes and Watson's reaction to their stories.

chronological arranged in the order of time in which events occurred

diction choice of words

flashback a narrative device in which the chronological order of the story is interrupted and events from an earlier time are presented

Writing about structure

Upgrade

You may be asked to write about language, form and structure.
Students often find writing about structure more difficult than writing about language, especially when considering how it affects meaning. However, even making basic observations, such as whether something occurs as part of the novel's climax or resolution could gain you vital marks. You may also earn marks for using correct terminology, such as 'exposition', 'sub-plot' or 'denouement'. Some structural points you may wish to consider are:

- What effect does Watson's narration have on the novel?

- What does the romantic sub-plot add to the novel?

- How does the short timescale of the novel increase its tension and excitement?

- Unusually, roughly halfway through the novel, Holmes names Jonathan Small as being responsible for Bartholomew's death. How does Conan Doyle maintain suspense for the rest of the novel?

- How effective is the lengthy last chapter in resolving the mystery?

Biography of Sir Arthur Conan Doyle

- Arthur was born in Edinburgh in 1859 to Charles, an artist, and Mary Doyle. He was the eldest of nine children.

- He enroled at the University of Edinburgh to study medicine in 1876, where he met Dr Joseph Bell, who inspired aspects of the character of Sherlock Holmes. Conan Doyle subsequently took over a medical practice in Southsea.

- In 1885, he married Mary Louise Hawkins, who may have been the model for the character of Mary Morstan in *The Sign of Four*.

- In 1887, 'A Study in Scarlet', the first of the Sherlock Holmes tales was published in *Beeton's Christmas Annual*. He also wrote a variety of other articles, stories and books, including historic romances.

Sir Arthur Conan Doyle (1859–1930)

- 'The Sign of the Four' was published in 1890 in *Lippincott's Monthly Magazine*. Conan Doyle left his medical practice.

- In 1892, a collection of Sherlock Holmes stories, *The Adventures of Sherlock Holmes*, was published. The next year, Conan Doyle decided to kill off Sherlock Holmes in order to concentrate on his more serious writing.

- In 1901, he wrote *The Hound of the Baskervilles*. The play *Sherlock Holmes* was successfully performed at the Lyceum Theatre, London. Conan Doyle resumed writing Sherlock Holmes stories.

- After an active life, including serving as a war correspondent, working in a hospital during the Boer War (South African War), running for Parliament and touring many foreign countries giving speeches, Conan Doyle died in 1930 and had a spiritualist funeral.

'Sherlock Holmes seems to have caught on.' (Arthur Conan Doyle in a letter to his mother, 1891)

Tips for assessment

Upgrade

Make sure when you use dates and other contextual facts that they are correct. Careless errors, such as writing '1990' rather than '1890' or 'Elizabethan era' rather than 'Victorian era', will cost you vital marks.

The Victorian era

The Victorian era refers to the period when Queen Victoria reigned, from 1837 to her death in 1901. This was a period of great technological and scientific advancement as well as the rapid growth of the British Empire. Arthur Conan Doyle's stories reflect a number of the concerns of the age.

Science and religion were increasingly seen to be at odds with each other and the publishing of Darwin's *On the Origin of Species* (1859) ignited many debates. Sherlock Holmes is seen by some as representing the supremacy of science over other beliefs and feelings, while Watson counters with his more sentimental and romantic attachments.

There was a public fascination with crime, such as the widely reported murders of 'Jack the Ripper', which took place in the Whitechapel district of London in 1888. Primitive **forensics** were being used, including analysis of crime scenes, autopsies and even basic crime scene photography. Holmes's analysis of the crime scene at Pondicherry Lodge is a demonstration of a scientific approach to a crime scene as opposed to Jones's more careless approach in which he simply arrests whoever is near at hand.

It was also a time when social advancement through enterprise or unexpected inheritance was desirable. While inherited land and property had once been the bedrock of social standing, valuable objects, sometimes acquired on adventures abroad, were now also seen as important. The fear of theft was a key feature of Victorian crime fiction. The significance of the treasure in *The Sign of Four* is even greater to Watson as he believes that Mary's acquisition of it could move her beyond his social sphere. She would become an heiress while he would remain a retired army surgeon on 'half-pay', which at that time would have been considered an unbridgeable social gap.

> **forensics** crime scene forensics involves the gathering of evidence, which can lead to the courtroom conviction of a criminal

Tips for assessment

Upgrade

When writing about the context of the novel, make sure that you are aware what percentage of the marks is awarded for contextual information. Contextual information should be woven into your response to show a greater understanding of the text rather than forming a lengthy separate section of your answer.

The British Empire

The Victorian age was one of great expansion for the British Empire and, by the end of the era, Britain ruled over almost a quarter of the world. In the latter half of the 19th century there was a particularly rapid expansion motivated by many factors, including competition with other European countries, the desire to generate greater wealth, the need for more foreign trading partners and a belief in the concept of a British Empire.

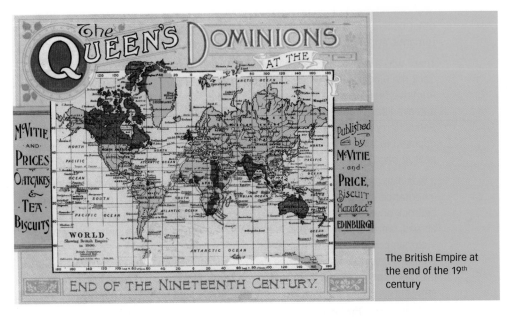

The British Empire at the end of the 19th century

In *The Sign of Four*, Conan Doyle refers particularly to the Indian Rebellion of 1857 when he has Jonathan Small mention 'the great mutiny'. This was an important uprising, which changed attitudes about the speed and manner of reform in India. Modern critics sometimes focus on the dangers and injustices of **imperialism** and **colonialism**, which feature in some 19th-century novels, including adventures in foreign territories. This critical approach is called **post-colonial criticism**. In *The Sign of Four*, Conan Doyle's depiction of the foreign characters is typical of the age. For example, his description of Tonga as a **"black cannibal"** and a **"savage"** (*Chapter 12*) or Small's account of India when **"two hundred thousand black devils let loose, and the country was perfect hell"** (*Chapter 12*) sound coarse and prejudiced to modern readers. However, they are in accord with the prevalent views and attitudes of the Victorian era when native populations were viewed as needing to be made 'British' in their tastes and habits, without any sensitivity to different customs and beliefs. For example, Small prefers India when it was **"still and peaceful, to all appearance, as Surrey or Kent"** (*Chapter 12*).

Additionally, some British subjects sought their fortunes in foreign countries, often at the cost of the native populations, and Conan Doyle exploits the possibilities for criminality and deceit, which haunt the criminals upon returning to England.

> **colonialism** the settling, transformation and restructuring of new territories
>
> **imperialism** the claiming and exploiting of new territories
>
> **post-colonial criticism** a type of literary criticism, which focuses both on texts by writers from nations, such as Britain, that colonized others, and on texts by writers from nations, such as India, that were colonized. It often questions the perspectives of the colonizers and seeks to discover alternative points of views. It explores concepts such as power, politics, religion and culture

Activity 1

Look closely at the exchange between Major Sholto and Jonathan Small in Chapter 12 from "None or all…" to "… that is, of Abdullah, Akbar, Mahomet, and myself.". Make a bullet point list noting the differences in attitude between Small and Sholto. What do these attitudes tell us about the men and the times in which they lived?

The role of women

The rights of women during the Victorian age were very restricted. They could not vote or own property in their own right and had limited employment opportunities. Women who worked often had to choose from a small range of jobs, such as being a governess, a seamstress or a servant. Women who did not hold jobs were often idealized for their contribution to Victorian family life as being 'the angel in the house'. In this role, they were praised for putting the needs of their husband above their own and, through 'passionate duty', creating a peaceful home.

Although Mary Morstan plays a significant role in *The Sign of Four*, she in many ways conforms to the Victorian ideal of gentleness and submission. She also chooses a gender-appropriate role of being a governess when her father dies without leaving her an inheritance. Watson remarks on her behaving **'after the angelic fashion of women'** shortly before she turns 'faint' and then bursts into a **'passion of weeping'** *(Chapter 7)*. However, her competence, intelligence and rationality are also praised and Holmes declares her **"a model client"** *(Chapter 2)*. The other female characters in the novel are landladies, such as Mrs Hudson, housekeepers like Mrs Bernstone, or wives, like Mrs Smith, with more limited roles than their adventurous male counterparts.

Key quotations

"I would not tell them too much," said Holmes. "Women are never to be entirely trusted – not the best of them." *(Chapter 9)*

"I should never marry myself, lest I bias my judgment." *(Chapter 12)*

Activity 2

- Consider Holmes's attitude towards women and compare and contrast it with Watson's. You may start with Chapter 2 and write a paragraph comparing Holmes's idea that Mary is a **'mere unit, a factor'** and Watson's more emotional response. Remember to pick out key quotations.

- Prepare a speech arguing for or against the following topic: Mary Morstan – early feminist or submissive female?

Victorian detective fiction

The American author and poet Edgar Allan Poe (1809–49) is largely credited with the invention of the detective story and Conan Doyle said that Poe's detective, M. Dupin, had 'from boyhood been one of my heroes'.

The first of the Dupin stories is 'The Murders in the Rue Morgue' (1841) in which an unnamed narrator marvels at the extraordinary analytical talents of his friend Dupin. The detective, through detailed observations of the crime scene, solves an apparently impossible **'locked room' murder** of two women, which has baffled the police. Like Holmes, Dupin takes a mathematical and analytical interest in the murders and avoids any emotional involvement in the nature of the crimes, however gruesome. Another influential detective novel is *The Moonstone* by Wilkie Collins, which, like *The Sign of Four*, has a 'locked room' murder and involves the robbery of a valuable foreign treasure. Collins established many of the conventions found in subsequent detective stories, such as **red herrings**, bungling local police and a twist in the plot. Charles Dickens (1812–70) focused on criminals in novels such as *Great Expectations* and *Oliver Twist*, but looks more particularly at detectives and the detection of crime in a sub-plot with Inspector Bucket in *Bleak House*.

> **'locked room' murder** a seemingly impossible murder, where, due to a door being locked from the inside, it is difficult to see how the murderer would have escaped
>
> **red herring** a clue that misleads the reader and encourages a false conclusion

Activity 3

Read the description below of Edgar Allan Poe's detective Dupin and then write a paragraph comparing his detective with Arthur Conan Doyle's Sherlock Holmes.

> He is fond of **enigmas**, of **conundrums**, of hieroglyphics; exhibiting in his solutions of each a degree of **acumen** which appears to the ordinary apprehension of the **preternatural**. His results, brought about by the very soul and essence of method, have, in truth, the whole air of **intuition**.

acumen cleverness or insight

conundrum a difficult riddle or puzzle

enigma something that is very puzzling and hard to understand

intuition arriving at a truth or solution without relying on reasoning; a quick insight

preternatural exceptional, abnormal or supernatural

The publishing history of Sherlock Holmes

Reading was a popular leisure activity during the Victorian era and there was a huge appetite for exciting, suspenseful stories. Conan Doyle was a young doctor who had financial responsibility for much of his family after the hospitalization of his father for alcoholism and epilepsy. He knew he had a talent for storytelling and felt that writing was a way of gaining additional financial security. He began selling a selection of articles, adventures and historic stories, his first being published when he was only 20.

Conan Doyle sold all the rights to his first Sherlock Holmes novel, *A Study in Scarlet*, for £25 in 1887 and it was published in a paperback annual magazine, *Beeton's Christmas Annual*. On the strength of it, he was invited, along with fellow author Oscar Wilde (1854–1900), to a dinner with Joseph Stoddart, the managing director of *Lippincott's Monthly Magazine*. Both authors were commissioned to produce a novel for that publication: Oscar Wilde's was *The Picture of Dorian Gray* and Conan Doyle's was *The Sign of Four*. It was originally published as *The Sign of the Four,* but Conan Doyle subsequently crossed out the 'the' and it went on to be published in other editions as *The Sign of Four*.

However, Sherlock Holmes's real popularity came with the publication of the short stories in *The Strand Magazine*. Books of the collected stories were then published and have remained widely read. Conan Doyle wearied of his most popular character and killed him off in 1893 in 'The Final Problem', only to be persuaded to resurrect him by publishers, the public and even his own mother. The final collection of Sherlock Holmes stories, *The Case-Book of Sherlock Holmes*, was published in 1927.

Activity 4

With a partner, turn to the next page and examine the cover of *Lippincott's Monthly Magazine* and discuss anything of interest that you notice about how Conan Doyle's story is advertised and what other stories and articles are in the same issue.

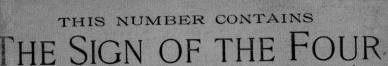

THIS NUMBER CONTAINS

THE SIGN OF THE FOUR

By A. CONAN DOYLE,

Author of "Micah Clarke: his Statement," etc.

COMPLETE. *Mrs Hammond*

FEBRUARY, 1890

LIPPINCOTT'S

MONTHLY MAGAZINE

CONTENTS

PRICE TWENTY-FIVE CENTS

J: B: LIPPINCOTT: Cᵒ: PHILADELPHIA:

LONDON: WARD, LOCK & CO.

PARIS: BRENTANO'S, 17 AVENUE DE L'OPÉRA.

Lippincott's Monthly Magazine was published in Philadelphia, USA
from 1868 to 1915

Writing about context

Upgrade

In the exam you may be asked to consider contexts outside the novel, although they will be relevant to the themes, characterization, language or plot within the novel. Some of the external contexts relevant to *The Sign of Four* you may like to consider are:

• To what extent does the portrayal of Mary Morstan represent Victorian ideals of womanhood?

• How do ideas of British Empire affect our understanding of the final chapter of the novel?

• What similarities does this novel have with other detective fiction of the 19th century?

• How do the characters of Watson and Holmes reflect the preoccupations of the Victorian era?

• What techniques does Conan Doyle use to create a piece of popular fiction appropriate for magazine readers?

Equally, the context in your exam question may come solely from something within the novel, such as a theme. Here are some examples of internal contexts you may write about:

• how Conan Doyle presents marriage in *The Sign of Four*

• the ways that Conan Doyle uses the geography and society of London in his story

• Conan Doyle's use of disguise and trickery

• how Conan Doyle contrasts Sherlock Holmes with Athelney Jones to bring out ideas about the police and justice

• the significance of the pearls in the story.

Main characters

Sherlock Holmes

Sherlock Holmes, the **"only unofficial consulting detective"** *(Chapter 1)*, is considered one of the most fascinating characters in literature and is essential to the lasting appeal of *The Sign of Four*. Conan Doyle said that his initial inspiration for the character was Dr Joseph Bell, who he studied under at the University of Edinburgh, but he also owes a debt to Dupin, Edgar Allan Poe's famous fictional detective, who shares some of Sherlock's eccentricities. The novel makes clear from the outset that there are two very different sides to Holmes: on the one hand, the easily bored and even depressed character that the reader first meets and, on the other, the brilliant, energetic detective solving apparently impossible cases. The reader is introduced to him when, shockingly, he is injecting himself with cocaine (an activity that was frowned upon but not illegal at the time) but rapidly sees his other side when he is given a problem to solve. The reader receives Holmes through Watson's admiring narration, so is led to share his appreciation of the detective, despite some of his more egotistical and unsympathetic tendencies. At the end of the novel, Holmes comments on his **duality** in the German extract from *Xenian,* suggesting that he is both a good man and a rogue ('Schelmen').

Sherlock Holmes, as played by Benedict Cumberbatch in the BBC's 'Sherlock' series

duality made up of two opposing parts, such as good and evil

empathy understanding and identification with the feelings, thoughts or actions of another

Key quotations

"There is something positively inhuman in you at times." *(Chapter 2)*

"Strange," said I, "how terms of what in another man I should call laziness alternate with your fits of splendid energy and vigour." *(Chapter 12)*

Activity 1

Read the excerpt below from an 1892 interview with Conan Doyle in which he describes Dr Joseph Bell. Then write a paragraph explaining the similarities between Dr Bell and Sherlock Holmes, using specific examples from *The Sign of Four*.

> Sherlock Holmes is the literary embodiment, if I may so express it, of my memory of a professor of medicine at Edinburgh University, who would sit in the patients' waiting-room with a face like a Red Indian and diagnose the people as they came in, before even they had opened their mouths. He would tell them their symptoms, he would give them details of their lives, and he would hardly ever make a mistake. "Gentlemen," he would say to us students standing around, "I am not quite sure whether this man is a cork-cutter or a slater. I observe a slight callus, or hardening, on one side of his thumb, and that is a sure sign he is either one or the other." His great faculty of deduction was at times highly dramatic. "Ah!" he would say to another man, "you are a soldier, a non-commissioned officer [NCO], and you have served in Bermuda. Now how did I know that, gentlemen? He came into our room without taking his hat off, as he would go into an orderly room. He was a soldier. A slight authoritative air, combined with his age, shows he was an NCO. A slight rash on the forehead tells me he was in Bermuda, and subject to a certain rash known only there." So I got the idea for Sherlock.

Activity 2

Write an opinion piece for a newspaper with the headline 'Sherlock Holmes: Hero or Rogue?', in which you explain whether you believe that the positive aspects of Holmes's personality outweigh the bad.

Doctor John Watson

Watson, a retired army surgeon who has returned from Afghanistan wounded, is Holmes's friend and biographer, as well as the narrator of the story. Despite their different habits and personalities, the men are close friends and Watson assists Holmes in the solving of crimes. Watson is a more conservative, measured character than Holmes and provides a bridge for the reader to Holmes's outrageous and brilliant escapades. It is interesting that Conan Doyle, himself a doctor, would choose that profession for Watson and some readers feel that Conan Doyle has a particular **empathy** with Watson.

Although he is a steadier character than Holmes, there are also indications that he is a man of the world. In Chapter 2, Watson refers to his 'experience of women which extends over many nations and three separate continents' and in Chapter 10, during the chase, he mentions hunting 'many creatures in many countries during my checkered career'. His involvement in Holmes's detection hints at his need for the 'wild thrill' (Chapter 10) that such adventures provide. In this novel, he is important not only as Holmes's sidekick, but also as the key figure in the romantic sub-plot with Mary Morstan. Watson's more romantic nature is frequently commented on by Holmes and is very apparent in the sections featuring Mary.

Key quotations

'What was I, an army surgeon with a weak leg and a weaker banking account, that I should dare to think of such things?' (Chapter 2)

"I have seen something of the rough side of life, but I give you my word that this quick succession of strange surprises tonight has shaken my nerve completely. I should like, however, to see the matter through with you, now that I have got so far." (Chapter 6)

Activity 3

Watson provides a number of hints about his life and career before he met Holmes. Make a list of these and then write a paragraph explaining how his personal history has influenced his character.

Activity 4

Imagine you have been asked to create a profile for Watson for a dating website. What would you put in this profile? Then do the same for the following characters:

- Sherlock Holmes
- Mary Morstan
- Thaddeus Sholto.

Compare your profiles with a partner. Discuss whose profile would be most successful and why.

Watson quickly falls in love with Mary Morstan, as played by Jude Law and Kelly Reilly in *Sherlock Holmes: A Game of Shadows*

Mary Morstan

Mary Morstan, introduced in Chapter 2, provides both the catalyst for the mystery and the love interest for the sub-plot. Although she is not described as possessing great beauty, her physical appearance suggests to Watson that her nature is 'spiritual', 'sympathetic', 'refined' and 'sensitive' *(Chapter 2)*. She demonstrates her intelligent and sensible nature in her relaying of the 'facts' of the case and by her calm reaction to the distressing events surrounding her father's death. However, she is also seen as someone who must be shielded from danger. She turns to Watson for 'comfort and protection' and is returned to Mrs Forrester's house at the first hint of any danger. Her love for Watson is demonstrated by her lack of interest in the treasure. Although Holmes regrets that Watson is marrying her, even he calls her "charming", "useful" and "a decided genius" *(Chapter 12)*.

Key quotations

'... I have never looked upon a face which gave a clearer promise of a refined and sensitive nature.' *(Chapter 2)*

'After the angelic fashion of women, she had borne trouble with a calm face as long as there was someone weaker than herself to support.' *(Chapter 2)*

 Activity 5

List some of the adjectives that are used to describe Mary Morstan in the novel. Using this list as a starting point, with a partner, discuss how Conan Doyle creates sympathy for her character.

 Activity 6

Compare the portrayal of Mary Morstan with that of the other female characters in the novel. You may start by comparing the difference between her reaction to the events of Pondicherry Lodge and that of Mrs Bernstone, the housekeeper, who is first introduced by the sound of 'the shrill, broken whimpering of a frightened woman' in Chapter 5. Other characters you could consider are Mrs Hudson, Mrs Forrester and Mrs Smith.

Thaddeus Sholto

Thaddeus is a colourful and amusing character, who, at a dramatic point in the story, also supplies a degree of comic relief. He is the son of Major Sholto and the twin brother of Batholomew Sholto, and has written the letter to Mary Morstan in order to ensure that she receives the inheritance that is due to her. Thaddeus's characteristics, including his **affectations** and eccentricities, were shared by some

affectation speech or behaviour that appears artificial, attention-seeking or designed to impress others

of the followers of the **Aesthetic Movement**. They believed that art should be decorative and beautiful rather than having any social or political meaning. Notable proponents of this movement included Aubrey Beardsley, Oscar Wilde and James McNeill Whistler. Thaddeus's room with its 'Eastern luxury', 'Oriental vase' and 'hookah' is rich with the Eastern art promoted by the Aesthetes (Chapter 4). Although Watson mocks his hypochondriac nature, Thaddeus is also sympathetically portrayed due to his honour in contacting Miss Morstan in order to return a portion of the treasure to her.

Key quotations

"I seldom come in contact with the rough crowd. I live, as you see, with some little atmosphere of elegance around me. I may call myself a patron of the arts." *(Chapter 4)*

"Besides, it would have been such bad taste to have treated a young lady in so scurvy a fashion." *(Chapter 4)*

Aesthetic Movement an arts movement in the latter half of the 19th century, which promoted 'art for art's sake'. Followers favoured highly decorative objects and were often influenced by exotic artefacts being brought into Europe at the time

Activity 7

Thaddeus and his twin brother Bartholomew, although physically similar, seem to have different personalities. Make a table comparing the two characters, including their very different reactions to the treasure.

Activity 8

Research the Aesthetic Movement and make a presentation in which you discuss the ways that you think Thaddeus conforms to this ideal. You may, for example, compare the description of Thaddeus's apartment with illustrations of rooms furnished in the style of the Aesthetic Movement. Use quotations from the text to support your arguments.

Tips for assessment

Upgrade

Remember when writing about characters that they are constructions of an author, not real people. You may find it useful to use phrases like 'Conan Doyle presents...' or 'the author suggests...' when writing about characters to emphasize the importance of the author's role.

Jonathan Small

Jonathan Small, a former soldier and prisoner, is one of the 'four', the group responsible for the theft of the disputed treasure. Holmes identifies him as one of the men involved in the murder of Major Sholto in Chapter 6 and provides a sceptical Jones with a detailed description of him. Small is the cause of Major Sholto's 'marked aversion to men with wooden legs' *(Chapter 4)* as Sholto recognizes him as the convict who he has previously betrayed. Small is clever and nearly evades Holmes, but is ultimately captured and tells his story. The reader may gain some sympathy for Small who is described as having a face that is not 'unpleasing' and showing 'something like humour in his eyes' *(Chapter 11)*. His life has been one of hardship, accidents, bad fortune and poor choices. Having left Worcestershire, as a bit of a 'rover' *(Chapter 12)*, he joined the army and headed for India, where, in a swimming accident, a crocodile bit off his leg. After a series of adventures, he agrees to collaborate with the other three members of the 'four' – two Sikh guards, Mahomet Singh and Abdullah Khan, and Dost Akbar, the travelling companion of the rajah's servant (who is disguised as a merchant) – in order to steal the rajah's treasure. After being captured and suffering many years in prison, he tries to gain freedom for the 'four' by bargaining with Major Sholto, who in turn betrays them all. Although implicated in the murders of the rajah's servant and Bartholomew Sholto, in both cases Small does not actually commit the murders and expresses regret about them. However, he admits to beating a convict-guard to death with his wooden leg, demonstrating his capacity for brutality. With his loyal companion Tonga, he seeks revenge for the major's betrayal, which ultimately is more important to him than the treasure, which he throws into the Thames.

> **Key quotations**
>
> "He is a poorly-educated man, small, active, with his right leg off, and wearing a wooden stump which is worn away upon the inner side." *(Chapter 6)*
>
> "I would rather swing a score of times, or have one of Tonga's darts in my hide, than live in a convict's cell and feel that another man is at his ease in a palace with the money that should be mine." *(Chapter 12)*

Activity 9

Many aspects of Small's life, as recounted in Chapter 12, read like an adventure tale. Imagine you have been asked to turn that chapter into a graphic novel or comic strip. Pick out the key lines and dialogue from Chapter 12 that you think would need to be presented. If time allows, draw the accompanying images.

Activity 10

Create a spider diagram with Jonathan Small's name in the centre. On the top half of the diagram put all the information the reader has learned about Small's appearance, actions and personality before Chapter 12 and on the bottom half everything the reader learns about him in Chapter 12. Decide if you have more sympathy for Small before or after the final chapter.

Athelney Jones

Jones is a police detective from Scotland Yard whose inefficient and unscientific approach to solving crimes is contrasted with Holmes's rational and knowledgeable one. The pitting of a conventional police officer against an unconventional, brilliant private detective is a common feature of detective stories and is frequently used not only in the stories of Conan Doyle but also those of well-known authors like Agatha Christie (1890–1976), whose novels featured the unlikely detectives Miss Marple and Hercule Poirot. Jones knows Holmes from a previous case, but is reluctant to give him credit for the investigation's success, saying **"you'll own now that it was more by good luck than good guidance"** *(Chapter 6)*. At one point, he is congratulated in a newspaper article for arresting most of the members of the Sholto household, who he is then embarrassingly forced to release. Holmes treats him with an amused **pragmatism**, devising ways of removing Jones from the location when he wishes to have the crime scene to himself or involving Jones in the chase when he wants the use of a police launch. Ironically, Jones thanks Holmes and Watson for their **"assistance"** when, as Watson remarks, Holmes has done **"all the work"** and **"Jones gets the credit"**. *(Chapter 12)*.

> **pragmatism** having a sensible and realistic attitude, with an understanding of what is possible and achievable

Key quotations

'He was red-faced, burly, and plethoric, with a pair of very small twinkling eyes which looked keenly out from between swollen and puffy pouches.' *(Chapter 6)*

"You are welcome to all the official credit, but you must act on the lines that I point out. Is that agreed?" *(Chapter 9)*

Activity 11

1. Imagine you are a casting director and you have been asked to cast an actor for the role of Jones. Write a casting brief for the role explaining:

   - what the character looks like
   - how he behaves
   - the qualities the actor playing the role will need
   - the character's importance in the novel.

2. Focusing on Bartholomew's death, write a paragraph comparing and contrasting Jones's and Holmes's reactions to the crime and the possible suspects.

Tips for assessment

When writing about characters look for changes and turning points in their characterizations. More developed characters will probably grow and change throughout the novel.

Minor characters

Tonga

Tonga is a member of one of the indigenous Andaman Island tribes, a group of people described in the novel as being **"the smallest race upon this earth"** and **"fierce, morose, and intractable"** *(Chapter 8)*. Different aspects of Tonga's character are highlighted. Watson emphasizes his cruelty and violence, describing his **'half animal fury'** and **'his strong yellow teeth gnashing at us'**. Even when disappearing beneath the waves to his death, his eyes are **'venomous, menacing'** *(Chapter 10)*.

However, Small presents a very different character. After Small nurses Tonga through a fever, Tonga became 'devoted' to him. He is loyal to Small, helps him to escape from the prison and allows himself to be exhibited as a **"black cannibal"** to support them both *(Chapter 12)*.

> **Key quotations**
>
> **'Never have I seen features so deeply marked with all bestiality and cruelty.'** *(Chapter 10)*
>
> **"He was staunch and true, was little Tonga. No man ever had a more faithful mate."** *(Chapter 12)*

Tonga has no dialogue in the text. With a partner, discuss why you think Conan Doyle did not write any dialogue for Tonga and if you would have viewed his character differently if he had spoken in the novel.

Mrs Hudson

Mrs Hudson is Sherlock Holmes's **'worthy'** landlady *(Chapter 9)*, who announces his visitors, worries about his welfare and demonstrates an almost motherly concern for him. She is dismayed by the boisterous entrance of the Baker Street Irregulars and by Holmes's radical mood changes.

Mrs Hudson, as played by Una Stubbs, in the BBC's 'Sherlock' series

Key quotations

"… but he turned on me, sir, with such a look that I don't know how ever I got out of the room." *(Chapter 9)*

Activity 13

1. With a partner, create a role-play in which Mrs Hudson describes her tenant Sherlock Holmes to one of her friends. Try to capture her attitude towards Holmes and her reactions to his visitors and habits.

2. Compare and contrast the portrayals of Mrs Cecil Forrester and Mrs Hudson in the novel. You may start with the sentence: 'Sherlock Holmes's landlady, Mrs Hudson, and Miss Morstan's employer, Mrs Cecil Forrester, are both respectable British women who are shown to be supportive and caring of others, yet they are also portrayed as leading very different lives.'

Tips for assessment

When writing about a text that has been adapted for film and TV, it is an easy mistake to write about what you think you know about the characters rather than what is actually written in the text. For example, although we may have an image of Sherlock Holmes wearing a deerstalker hat or Mrs Hudson being an elderly woman, there is no evidence of either of these notions in *The Sign of Four*. Make sure you can support your characterization points by what is actually in the text and not what you have seen on the screen.

Major Sholto

Major Sholto is an army officer who served in India and returned a rich man. He is the father of the twins Thaddeus and Bartholomew and is first mentioned in Chapter 2 as Captain Morstan's only friend in London. Holmes connects the death of Sholto four years after the disappearance of Morstan with the first mysterious annual present of a pearl to Miss Morstan. Sholto felt guilty about his **"treatment of poor Morstan's orphan"** *(Chapter 4)* and wanted to make amends, but died before he could tell his sons where the treasure was hidden. A more negative portrayal of Sholto appears in Chapter 12, when he is revealed as an unsuccessful gambler, a disloyal friend and a thief. Sholto is haunted by his evil deeds and pursued by Small, who is seeking vengeance upon him.

> **Key quotations**
>
> "The cursed greed which has been my besetting sin through life has withheld from her the treasure, half at least of which should have been hers. And yet I have made no use of it myself, so blind and foolish a thing is avarice." *(Chapter 4)*
>
> "Major Sholto was the hardest hit… All day he would wander about as black as thunder, and he took to drinking a deal more than was good for him." *(Chapter 12)*

> **Activity 14**
>
> 1. Major Sholto says that greed has been his 'besetting sin' throughout life. What evidence is there in the novel that his life has been ruined by greed? Write a paragraph explaining your opinion with evidence from the novel.
>
> 2. One of the themes of the novel is friendship. What does the reader learn about Major Sholto's attitude towards friends?

Bartholomew Sholto

Bartholomew is Thaddeus Sholto's clever but less honourable twin brother, who is discovered dead in Chapter 5. Obsessed with discovering his father's hidden treasure he spent years digging up the grounds of Pondicherry Lodge. While Thaddeus thought they should share their wealth with Mary Morstan, **"Brother Bartholomew could not altogether see it in that light"** *(Chapter 4)*. Upon discovering the treasure, however, Bartholomew dies a terrible death.

> **Key quotations**
>
> **"Bartholomew is a clever fellow…"** *(Chapter 4)*
>
> 'The features were set, however, in a horrible smile, a fixed, unnatural grin…' *(Chapter 5)*

Activity 15

Bartholomew's death is a shock to the other characters, but he does not seem to be particularly loved or mourned. With a partner, discuss why Conan Doyle may have chosen to avoid the reader having a great deal of affection for Bartholomew.

Captain Morstan

Captain Morstan's mysterious disappearance is an important plot element. The reader learns about him through the recollections of his daughter Mary, Major Sholto and Jonathan Small. These three different witnesses suggest a complex and flawed character. Although she was sent away to boarding school when she was a child (not an uncommon occurrence for the children of army officers at this time), so perhaps did not know her father well, Mary tells of receiving a message **"full of kindness and love"** from him *(Chapter 2)*. In contrast, he is portrayed as the gambling and drinking friend of Major Sholto, with whom he is seen **"stumbling along on the way to their quarters"** *(Chapter 12)*. Although he may have a few more scruples than the major, acknowledging that Small's plan is **"dirty business"** *(Chapter 12)*, he agrees to it in order to avoid financial embarrassment and disgrace and does nothing to honour his side of his agreement with Small. The reader may feel that Morstan's true nature remains something of a mystery.

> **Key quotations**
>
> **"My father was an officer in an Indian regiment, who sent me home when I was quite a child. My mother was dead, and I had no relative in England. I was placed, however, in a comfortable boarding establishment at Edinburgh…"** *(Chapter 2)*
>
> **"It's a dirty business,"** the other answered. **"Yet, as you say, the money will save our commissions handsomely."** *(Chapter 12)*

Based on the information that can be found in the novel about Captain Morstan, write an obituary for him containing the main events in his life.

Wiggins

Wiggins is the young leader of the Baker Street Irregulars, who Holmes employs on occasional errands. He bears some resemblance to the Artful Dodger in Charles Dickens's *Oliver Twist* (1838), who is also the leader of a group of poor London boys. He is a keen negotiator and maintains a certain dignity despite his disreputable appearance.

Key quotations

'One of their number, taller and older than the others, stood forward with an air of lounging superiority which was very funny in such a disreputable little scarecrow.' *(Chapter 8)*

Activity 17

Wiggins is one of a number of interesting visitors to the Baker Street flat. How does Conan Doyle make clear that he is an unusual guest? Compare his entrance to Holmes's rooms with those of the following characters and explain what Conan Doyle reveals about each of these characters by their entrances:

- Miss Morstan *(Chapter 2)*
- Mr Jones *(Chapter 9)*
- The old sailor (Holmes in disguise) *(Chapter 9)*.

Mordecai Smith

Smith agrees to rent his steam launch, the *Aurora*, to Small and Tonga. He apparently likes a drink as he is said to be **'the worse for liquor'** *(Chapter 10)* and will do whatever Small asks in return for money and alcohol. When arrested, Small absolves him of any guilt and he is unlikely to go to prison.

Key quotations

"As long as he has liquor and good pay, why should he ask questions?" *(Chapter 10)*

"If we are pretty quick in catching our men, we are not so quick at condemning them." *(Chapter 11)*

Mrs Smith

Mrs Smith is the wife of Mordecai Smith, the boat owner, and mother to Jack, the "rosy-cheeked young rascal" with whom Holmes converses *(Chapter 8)*. She is portrayed as a busy, somewhat exasperated, wife and mother. She is tricked by Holmes into providing a detailed description of the *Aurora*.

> **Key quotations**
>
> '... a stoutish, red-faced woman with a large sponge in her hand.' *(Chapter 8)*
>
> "My old man woke up Jim – that's my eldest – and away they went without so much as a word to me." *(Chapter 8)*

Activity 18

1. How does Holmes trick Mrs Smith into revealing all she knows about Small and the boat? With a partner, create a role-play in which you try to get information from each other using similar techniques.

2. What do we learn about the family life of the Smiths from Holmes's encounter with Mrs Smith? Consider:

   - the behaviour and attitude of the children
   - Smith's work and attitude
   - Mrs Smith's concerns and priorities.

Mrs Cecil Forrester

Mrs Forrester employs Miss Morstan as a governess. Mrs Forrester's life is depicted as a very comfortable one where her children are looked after by a governess and servants take care of the other duties. She is also a friend and confidante to Miss Morstan and Watson is pleased to see that Miss Morstan is 'no mere paid dependant but an honoured friend' *(Chapter 7)*. She portrays many of the homely and feminine qualities admired by Watson. Her home is idealized as 'a tranquil English home in the midst of the wild, dark business which had absorbed us' *(Chapter 7)*. With her eager curiosity about the outcome of the mystery, she could be seen as representative of the many readers of the Sherlock Holmes stories.

> **Key quotations**
>
> "It is a romance!" cried Mrs Forrester. "An injured lady, half a million in treasure, a black cannibal, and a wooden-legged ruffian. They take the place of the conventional dragon or wicked earl." *(Chapter 9)*

McMurdo

McMurdo is a former prize-fighter who now works at Pondicherry Lodge making sure that no unwanted visitors are admitted. He is delighted to see Sherlock Holmes, who had fought him four years previously at his 'benefit', a charity fight where the proceeds went to the nominated fighter.

> **Key quotations**
>
> "You might have aimed high, if you had joined the fancy." *(Chapter 5)*

Activity 19

What does the reader learn about Sherlock Holmes through his conversation with McMurdo?

Tips for assessment

There are many opportunities to focus on how dialogue is used to establish characters in the novel. For example, McMurdo's distinctive manner of speaking and the change in his attitude and dialogue once he recognizes Sherlock Holmes makes him a more vivid and distinct character.

Mr Sherman

Sherman is Holmes's naturalist acquaintance who keeps a variety of animals. Like McMurdo, he provides another distinctive working-class character and shows the broad range of acquaintances that Holmes has acquired through his many adventures.

> **Key quotations**
>
> '… I could see dimly that there were glancing, glimmering eyes peeping down at us from every cranny and corner.' *(Chapter 7)*

Activity 20

There are a number of working-class characters in the novel who play small but important roles. With your group, have a discussion about how Holmes has met and maintained an acquaintance with the following characters:

- Mr Sherman
- Mrs Smith
- McMurdo.

In your discussion try to reach a conclusion about whether he keeps in touch only with those who he thinks will be of value to him or if there is any evidence of actual friendships. Do you think that Holmes has the ability to form close emotional attachments?

Toby

Toby is the dog with a keen sense of smell who helps to track down Small and Tonga.

Key quotations

'... an ugly, long-haired, lop-eared creature, half spaniel and half lurcher, brown and white in colour, with a very clumsy, waddling gait...'
(Chapter 7)

Activity 21

In Chapter 7, Watson and Holmes's journey across south London, led by the keen Toby, provides the opportunity for Holmes to fill Watson (and the reader) in on a number of important plot points. What does Toby's presence add to this chapter?

Writing about characters

Upgrade

If you can demonstrate in your exam that you have an understanding of characterization, this will aid you in discussing the themes and ideas in the text. For example, if you explain how a character is portrayed sympathetically or critically, you will be able to show how the author is promoting certain ideas or values.

Considering the following will help you answer character-based questions in your exam:

- What are your first impressions of this character and how do they change throughout the novel?
- What techniques does the author use to make this character sympathetic/frightening/comic?
- How are the character's thoughts and feelings portrayed?
- How is the relationship of this character with another character portrayed in the novel?
- What attitudes does this character show towards friendship/money/adventure?
- How does this character develop and change throughout the novel?
- Is this character a reliable narrator or are they biased/self-serving?
- How does the language used by this character reveal his/her personality?
- What is the importance of this character to the plot of the novel?

Character map

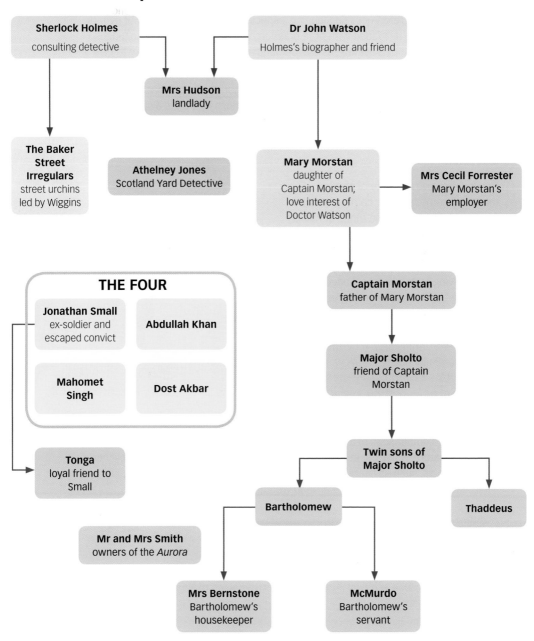

Sherlock Holmes
consulting detective

Dr John Watson
Holmes's biographer and friend

Mrs Hudson
landlady

The Baker Street Irregulars
street urchins led by Wiggins

Athelney Jones
Scotland Yard Detective

Mary Morstan
daughter of Captain Morstan; love interest of Doctor Watson

Mrs Cecil Forrester
Mary Morstan's employer

THE FOUR

Jonathan Small
ex-soldier and escaped convict

Abdullah Khan

Mahomet Singh

Dost Akbar

Tonga
loyal friend to Small

Captain Morstan
father of Mary Morstan

Major Sholto
friend of Captain Morstan

Twin sons of Major Sholto

Bartholomew

Thaddeus

Mr and Mrs Smith
owners of the *Aurora*

Mrs Bernstone
Bartholomew's housekeeper

McMurdo
Bartholomew's servant

Although Conan Doyle was writing popular fiction, some modern readers may find his vocabulary and references challenging, especially when he writes about events whose significance has faded with time or when he lapses into foreign languages. However, it is worth persevering, as this demanding language is necessary to give a rounded portrayal of the educated and brilliant Holmes.

Just as Holmes has an outstanding eye for detail, Conan Doyle is a master of description and deftly brings his characters and locations to life. He also uses a variety of techniques to create suspense and humour.

Simile

Conan Doyle uses a range of **similes** in the novel, sometimes for comic effect. For example, he describes the fringe of hair on Thaddeus Sholto's head and the bald scalp, which 'shot out from among it like a mountain-peak from fir-trees' *(Chapter 4)*. Upon arriving at Pondicherry Lodge and seeing that the grounds have been dug up, Watson remarks that it looks 'as though all the moles in England had been let loose in it' *(Chapter 5)*. Amusingly, Toby, the dog with the extraordinary ability to follow a scent is depicted 'like a connoisseur sniffing the bouquet of a famous vintage' *(Chapter 7)*. In all of these instances, Conan Doyle is creating vivid and dramatic descriptions by making exaggerated comparisons of a somewhat humorous nature.

Toby the dog is likened to a connoisseur sniffing a famous vintage

However, in Jonathan Small's narrative, similes are more clichéd and predictable, such as 'running like the wind' *(Chapter 12)*, suggesting that he is a less literate and educated speaker than Watson.

> **simile** a comparison of one thing to another, using 'like' or 'as'

Activity 1

With a partner, look at the examples of similes below and explain the effect they have on the reader:

- 'This Agra treasure intervened like an impassable barrier between us.' *(Chapter 7)*
- '… to drag him, like some evil fish, over our side.' *(Chapter 10)*
- '… he followed him like his shadow.' *(Chapter 12)*

Metaphor

Metaphor is used to create some striking effects in the novel. When Holmes declares that a client is **'a mere unit, a factor in a problem'** *(Chapter 2)*, this choice of words underlines his cold, mathematical reasoning. Thaddeus Sholto describes his home as an **'oasis of art in the howling desert of South London'** *(Chapter 4)*. The word 'oasis' seems both exotic and peaceful, while a 'howling desert' depicts a despairing, lonely place. The creative exaggeration of this metaphor suits the artful nature of Thaddeus and highlights how out of place his apartment is in its unpromising location of a **'third-rate suburban dwelling house'** *(Chapter 3)*. Another interesting use of metaphor is the 'treasure' in Chapter 11. Although a literal treasure has been lost, Watson declares Mary a metaphorical treasure when he states, **'Whoever had lost a treasure, I knew that night I had gained one'** *(Chapter 11)*. Although this shows that Mary has great value to him, it could also be argued that this suggests that she has become his possession.

> **alliteration** the use of the same first letter or sound in words that are next to one another or very closely grouped together
>
> **metaphor** a comparison of one thing to another to make a description more vivid; unlike a simile, it does not use the words 'like' or 'as', but states that something is something else

Activity 2

Watson declares that Holmes really is 'an automaton – a calculating machine' *(Chapter 2)*. With a partner, discuss what he means by this metaphor. Then write a list of other metaphors Watson could have used to achieve a similar effect.

Tips for assessment

When writing about language ensure you make clear that the author is using specific literary techniques in order to create particular effects. Use phrases like 'Conan Doyle's use of alliteration highlights…' or 'Conan Doyle is clearly being ironic when he writes…'.

Alliteration

Conan Doyle employs **alliteration** throughout the novel, noting on the first page Holmes's **'masterly manner'**. The use of alliteration highlights the literary quality of Watson's accounts, which Holmes dismisses as being tinged with 'romanticism'. When conjuring the unfavourable London weather in Chapter 3, Watson uses a series of words beginning with 'd': 'dreary', 'dense, drizzly', 'drooped', stressing the heavy, depressing nature of the scene. At the end of Chapter 8, Watson is sent to sleep on a series of gentle 's' words and **'floated peacefully away upon a soft sea of sound'** *(Chapter 8)*, ending with the 'sweet' face of Mary Morstan. The recurring 's' sounds suggest the rhythmic breaths of someone falling into slumber. Jonathan Small describes the **'fat, frightened face'** of the merchant Achmet moments before his death *(Chapter 12)*. This harsh alliteration makes Achmet seem more pathetic and emphasizes the cruelty of Small's actions.

A more humorous use of alliteration is evident in Jones's labelling Holmes **'a connoisseur of crime'** *(Chapter 12)*, as the word 'connoisseur' is usually applied to being an expert in fine wines, food or art (as Thaddeus describes himself), rather than theft and murder. It may also remind the reader that the last time that word was used in the novel was when it was applied to Toby the dog, so it is perhaps not entirely flattering to Holmes.

> **Key quotations**
>
> "I have coursed many creatures in many countries during my checkered career..." *(Chapter 10)*

Activity 3

1. **a)** Look at the following excerpts from the novel and insert the correct alliterative word in each:
    - '... the day had been a dreary one, and a ____drizzly fog lay low upon the great city.' *(Chapter 3)*
    - '... our imaginations had conjured up that wild, _____ face.' *(Chapter 4)*
    - "You see I am weaving my ____ round Thaddeus." *(Chapter 6)*

    b) Now for each excerpt, explain what effect the use of alliteration has on the image that Conan Doyle creates.

2. Now create your own alliterative descriptions of at least three of the characters in the novel, e.g. 'loyal, long-suffering, literate Watson'.

Animal imagery

Conan Doyle makes striking use of animals and animal **imagery** in *The Sign of Four*. Notably, there is a degree of **anthropomorphism** or **personification** in the depiction of Toby, the 'inimitable' dog with the keen scent, when he is described as having **'a most comical cock'** to his head, **'like a connoisseur sniffing the bouquet of a famous vintage'** *(Chapter 7)*. Later, he is **'the very picture of canine indecision'**, looking **'as if to ask for sympathy in his embarrassment'** *(Chapter 7)*. This expression of subtle dog emotions provides Toby with a humanity beyond that of an ordinary sniffer dog.

Basil Rathbone, who played Holmes in a famous 1939 film, looking rather hawk-like with his chiselled features and cape

However, more frequently, Conan Doyle compares humans to animals. Holmes is noted for his 'clear-cut, hawk-like features' *(Chapter 2)* and later is compared both to a bird and a bloodhound when he is engaged in examining the crime scene with his 'beady eyes gleaming and deep-set like those of a bird' whereas his movements are 'like those of a trained bloodhound' *(Chapter 6)*. When making a discovery he 'broke out into a loud crow of delight' *(Chapter 6)*. These images are used not to demean Holmes's talents but to suggest his enormous energy and to make it clear that his senses are more highly developed than the average human's – he sees as sharply as a hawk and can follow a scent like a hound.

anthropomorphism attributing human characteristics to an animal or object

imagery the use of visual or other vivid language to convey ideas or emotions

pathetic fallacy the assigning of human emotions to aspects of nature, such as 'laughing sunlight' or 'cruel rain'

personification when human qualities are given to something non-human, such as an object or idea

Activity 4

1. Who is described as being able to 'climb like a cat' and 'strutting about as proud as a peacock' *(Chapter 12)*? What do these alliterative similes tell us about this character?

2. In Chapter 10, Holmes exclaims, "A strange enigma is man!" and Watson replies, "Someone calls him a soul concealed in an animal." With a partner, discuss what you think Watson means and how these ideas may relate to the novel.

Pathetic fallacy

Like many mystery writers, Conan Doyle creates a strong sense of place. Within his descriptions of locations, he also uses **pathetic fallacy** to heighten the mood. On the eerie trip to the Lyceum Theatre the dreariness and unease of their journey is increased by his description of the 'Mud-coloured clouds', which 'drooped sadly over the muddy streets' *(Chapter 3)*. The 'dull, heavy evening' combined with their 'strange business' makes Watson 'nervous and depressed' *(Chapter 3)*.

Watson's reaction to his surroundings increases the reader's state of tension. In Chapter 10, Jonathan Small's desperate plight is emphasized when he finds himself stranded in a 'wild and desolate' place, which eventually captures him within its 'sodden soil' *(Chapter 12)*. In each instance the description of nature reflects and enhances the emotional state of the characters.

Key quotations

"Was ever such a dreary, dismal, unprofitable world? See how the yellow fog swirls down the street and drifts across the dun-coloured houses. What could be more hopelessly prosaic and material?" *(Chapter 1)*

'There was, to my mind, something eerie and ghost-like in the endless procession of faces which flitted across these narrow bars of light – sad faces and glad, haggard and merry. Like all humankind, they flitted from the gloom into the light, and so back into the gloom once more.' *(Chapter 3)*

'The whole place, with its scattered dirt-heaps and ill-grown shrubs, had a blighted, ill-omened look which harmonized with the black tragedy which hung over it.' *(Chapter 7)*

Tips for assessment

Remember not just to note when pathetic fallacy occurs but also to consider how Conan Doyle uses it to create a specific mood or atmosphere.

Irony

There is clear irony in the fact that it is bumbling Jones who is described in the newspaper as having "a single vigorous and masterful mind" rather than the far more deserving Holmes *(Chapter 8)*. Watson also ironically comments on Jones's many wrongful arrests, saying 'we have had a close shave ourselves of being arrested for the crime' *(Chapter 8)*. Irony is used in the novel to show the difference between how the crime is actually solved and the incorrect perceptions of others.

There are also examples of **sarcasm**, such as when Holmes describes the murderous habits of the aborigines of the Andaman Islands in Chapter 8 and concludes, "Nice, amiable people, Watson!" Conan Doyle is also being ironic when he has Holmes criticize Watson's writing, comparing it to a 'love-story' and lacking a sense of 'proportion', since Watson's story and Conan Doyle's are the same. Conan Doyle is playfully advertising his previous novel *A Study in Scarlet*, but instead of promoting its virtues he ironically chooses to have Holmes disregard it, while still encouraging the reader's interest.

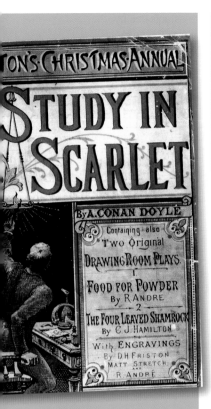

A Study in Scarlet, as seen on
Beeton's Christmas Annual in 1887

Key quotations

"Isn't it gorgeous!" said Holmes, grinning over his coffee cup. "What do you think of it?" *(Chapter 8)*

"I think that we have had a close shave ourselves of being arrested for the crime." *(Chapter 8)*

"So do I. I wouldn't answer for our safety now, if he should happen to have another of his attacks of energy." *(Chapter 8)*

Activity 5

Carefully read the two newspaper accounts of the Pondicherry Lodge crime, in Chapters 8 and 9, and note any examples of irony. Then:

a) Complete the following sentence: 'Conan Doyle includes the newspaper reports of the crime in order to…'

b) Using irony, write your own newspaper account about the final solution to the crime in the style of these articles.

Dialogue and dialect

Aware of the Victorian preoccupation with social class, Conan Doyle carefully signposts the backgrounds of his characters with his **dialogue**. He differentiates the dialogue of the characters by making the diction and **syntax** specific to that character. Thaddeus Sholto's very distinct character is established not only by his detailed physical description but his unique way of speaking with repetitions, questions and interrupted thoughts (represented by the dashes). His rather self-centred and hypochondriac nature is further suggested by his repetition of the

dialogue the speeches or conversations in a book or play

sarcasm a type of irony, using words to mean the opposite of what is said, often creating either a comic or insulting effect

syntax the structure of sentences, including word order and grammar

word 'I' and his use of medical terminology. Other characters are established by regional **dialect** or by a **sociolect**, which indicates their social class. The prize-fighter McMurdo reveals his background with his use of 'hain't' and 'o' ' as well as his boxing terminology like 'cross-hit' and 'fancy'. When Holmes decides to disguise himself as an old sailor he also disguises his voice by assuming a working-class sociolect with 'ain't' and 'an' ', and then drops his disguise by returning to his own voice and asking for a cigar.

> **dialect** particular pronunciations and word choices used by people of a particular geographical region
>
> **sociolect** particular pronunciations and word choices used by people of a particular social class

Activity 6

Read the exchange between Wiggins, the leader of the Baker Street Irregulars, and Holmes in Chapter 8. Then write a paragraph explaining what we learn about the character of Wiggins through his dialogue.

Activity 7

Conan Doyle provides an insight into his characters by giving them very distinctive ways of speaking. Look at the quotations below and identify which character is speaking and what is interesting about their choice of words.

- "Was ever such a dreary, dismal, unprofitable world?" *(Chapter 1)*
- "… if we can get the better of Brother Bartholomew." *(Chapter 4)*
- "Yes, sir, a brown, monkey-faced chap that's called more'n once for my old man." *(Chapter 8)*
- "Keep clear of the badger, for he bites. Ah naughty, naughty!" *(Chapter 7)*
- "Because I love you, Mary, as truly as ever a man loved a woman." *(Chapter 11)*
- "Folk may be friends o' yours, and yet no friends o' the masters." *(Chapter 5)*

Writing about language

Upgrade

In order to achieve high marks in your exam, you must demonstrate that you understand how Conan Doyle uses specific literary techniques in order to achieve his results. It is not enough to simply embed quotations into your responses. You must show that you understand the effects of his word choices.

Below are some tips on how to prepare to write about language:

- Make specific notes on the dialogue of the characters. Note when a particular syntax or diction are used.

- Note the use of the narrator and how that influences the way the reader receives the story.

- Show an awareness of the role of the writer. Use phrases like 'Conan Doyle contrasts...', 'Conan Doyle creates...' or 'Conan Doyle suggests...'.

- Pick out short quotations to support your points. It may be worth memorizing key quotations so you do not need to search for them during the exam.

- Be aware of when the text may be interpreted in more than one way or when a modern reader may perceive a text differently from a Victorian reader.

- Use literary terminology correctly. However, don't just list techniques. You must explain the effect that is being created.

- Be sensitive to changes in mood and atmosphere in the text and consider how the author achieves this.

- Highlight the use of contrasts, e.g. comedy versus horror, or romance versus science.

Given the exciting nature of a detective story, it is easy to forget that Conan Doyle is developing a series of themes throughout the novel, such as friendship, crime and duality. As you read the novel, note when a key theme is being presented and developed, and consider how Conan Doyle influences our opinions of these themes by his presentation of them.

Crime and punishment

At the heart of most detective stories is a crime and several are presented in *The Sign of Four*. The crimes and mysteries explored include:

- the theft of the rajah's treasure
- the murder of the rajah's servant
- the disappearance, death and disposal of Captain Morstan
- the murder of Bartholomew Sholto and theft of the treasure
- the murder of the convict-guard.

In the novel, the emphasis is more on the detection of the crime than the plight of the victim. For example, despite the description of his grotesque death, the reader is invited to have little sympathy for Bartholomew, as Watson remarks, **'I had heard little good of him and could feel no intense antipathy to his murderers'** *(Chapter 8)*. He also feels a certain ambiguity about the recovery of the treasure. Although he feels it belongs 'rightfully' to Miss Morstan, he is very grateful when it disappears as it means that her wealth is no longer a barrier to their forming a romantic relationship.

Those who commit crimes in the novel are often punished, although not always through the legal process. Major Sholto is punished by living a life perpetually fearing an attack. Bartholomew is punished for his greed and reluctance to share the inheritance by a grisly death. Tonga is punished for the murder of Bartholomew when shot by Holmes and Watson. However, Jonathan Small is a character who is punished by the law, first for his role in the initial theft and murder and then for his role in the second theft and murder. His reaction to his final capture, after an initial period of fury, is quite matter of fact, stating that he bears **"no grudge"** and that it is **"all fair and above-board"** *(Chapter 12)*. He is then given a full opportunity to tell his story from his point of view and the reader may ultimately feel more sympathy for him than the dead Major Sholto.

Love and friendship

One aspect of the lasting appeal of the Sherlock Holmes tales is Conan Doyle's presentation of the friendship between Watson and Holmes. This enduring relationship, where Watson's stolid reliability is countered by Holmes's brilliance and changeability, is at the centre of the novel. It begins and ends with the two

Activity 1

1. Carefully reread the description of the theft and murder of the rajah's servant in Chapter 12, making particular note of any words or phrases that may make the reader sympathetic to the servant. For example, what is the effect of the simile **'like a mouse'** or the description that he was **'in a quiver with fear'** *(Chapter 12)*? Then read the description of the theft and murder of Bartholmew Sholto. Write a paragraph comparing and contrasting Conan Doyle's depiction of these two victims.

2. 'In *The Sign of Four* crime does not pay.' Write and deliver a two-minute speech in which you either agree or disagree with this statement, using clear evidence from the text to support your point of view.

Jude Law and Robert Downey Junior characterize the relationship between Watson and Holmes in the 2009 film

men demonstrating both the depth of their friendship and their differences, as Watson, although constantly expressing admiration for Holmes, is 'hurt' by Holmes's insensitivity both to the fate of his brother in the first chapter and his impending marriage in the last. In both instances this friction is caused by Sherlock Holmes's rejection of conventional emotion.

On the other hand, Conan Doyle portrays Watson as being highly susceptible to emotion and he appears to fall in love with Mary Morstan almost upon first sight, not for her great beauty, but for her **'refined and sensitive nature'** *(Chapter 2)*. After her departure from their first meeting, he muses on the impossibility of their marriage, feeling unworthy of her. By that night, he finds himself passionately in love with her, while always maintaining a high degree of **decorum** and respect. The novel ends with an engagement that, although **foreshadowed** throughout the novel, is unconventional due to its speed. On the other hand, Sherlock Holmes is presented as being immune to love and actually objects to Watson's marriage, declaring, **"I should never marry myself"** *(Chapter 12)*.

Other examples of friendship in the novel include that between Small and Tonga and between Major Sholto and Captain Morstan, although these are both presented as flawed relationships that lead to crime. The bond between Small and Tonga is strong, but it is not a relationship of equals. Tonga serves Small and helps him to pursue

decorum proper, dignified and socially acceptable behaviour

foreshadowing a literary device in which the author hints at what will happen at a later point

his revenge. Sholto and Morstan's friendship is more equal and is based on casual drinking and ruinous gambling, leading to their involvement in stealing the treasure. Sholto then betrays Morstan by refusing to share the treasure with him. It could be argued that Conan Doyle presents Small as the more loyal friend, not only for his regard for Tonga but also for the loyalty that he demonstrates to the rest of the 'Four', who he refuses to betray, perhaps as an example of honour among thieves.

Whatever the flaws in the relationship between Holmes and Watson, the reader is likely to think positively of their friendship as it ultimately leads to the solving of crimes, as opposed to the friendships motivated by self-interest and greed.

> **Key quotations**
>
> 'A wondrous subtle thing is love, for here were we two, who had never seen each other before that day, between whom no word or even look of affection had ever passed, and yet now in an hour of trouble our hands instinctively sought for each other.' *(Chapter 5)*
>
> 'True, if I found it, it would probably put her forever beyond my reach. Yet it would be a petty and selfish love which would be influenced by such a thought as that.' *(Chapter 8)*
>
> "But love is an emotional thing, and whatever is emotional is opposed to that true cold reason which I place above all things." *(Chapter 12)*

> **Activity 2**
>
> Write a paragraph contrasting the different attitudes towards friendship demonstrated by Jonathan Small and Major Sholto.

> **Tips for assessment**
>
> When writing about themes use phrases such as 'Conan Doyle presents the theme of friendship by…' or 'The theme of wealth is important to the plot of the novel because…'.

Wealth and treasure

The receipt of a single valuable pearl begins the mystery for Mary Morstan and consequently for Holmes and Watson. The pearls, which are sent singly and at regular intervals without any explanation, intrigue the reader and provide a more exotic and exciting aspect to the enquiry.

In response to a mysterious letter, the three are led to another exotic treasure, the contents of Thaddeus Sholto's apartment. Conan Doyle enthusiastically describes the

Mary Morstan receives a number of valuable pearls

surroundings, emphasizing their opulence and exotic qualities: **'the suggestion of Eastern luxury'**, **'Two great tiger-skins'**, **'some richly mounted painting or Oriental vase'** *(Chapter 4)*. Although Thaddeus is shown enjoying his treasures, albeit in a somewhat solitary and eccentric way, his father and brother have had a very different experience of their wealth. His father declares on his deathbed that **'cursed greed'** has been **'my besetting sin through life'** and wishes to make reparation *(Chapter 4)*. His brother Bartholomew also pays with his life, years of which have been spent obsessively pursuing the hidden treasure, by being killed by Tonga when he and Small steal it.

Ultimately, the treasure is treated rather off-handedly, being tossed into the Thames by Small rather than **'let it go to kith or kin of Sholto or Morstan'** *(Chapter 12)*. The treasure almost seems to be cursed, bringing only unhappiness to the rajah's servant, the Sholtos and the 'Four', including Small. The idea that this treasure is not truly worth having is reinforced when Watson and Mary are relieved at its disappearance and Watson celebrates Mary as being his real 'treasure'.

Key quotations

"**They have been pronounced by an expert to be of a rare variety and of considerable value.**" *(Chapter 2)*

Activity 3

Copy this diagram. Then find evidence for the attitude towards wealth displayed by each of these characters and add it to your diagram.

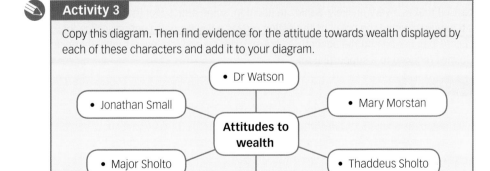

- Dr Watson
- Jonathan Small
- Mary Morstan
- **Attitudes to wealth**
- Major Sholto
- Thaddeus Sholto
- Bartholomew Sholto

Englishness and foreignness

Most of the novel takes place in London and its near surroundings with Conan Doyle conjuring the locations precisely, such as Holmes's flat on Baker Street; the trip to the Lyceum Theatre in the busy West End; the mysterious journey out to the suburbs to Thaddeus Sholto's apartment and then on to Pondicherry Lodge; the walk across south London with Toby the dog; and the chase down the Thames in the police launch. Mrs Forrester's Camberwell home, with its servants and **'soft light of a shaded lamp'** *(Chapter 11)*, is idealized as a **'tranquil English home'** *(Chapter 7)*, which is a refuge from the external dangers that surround the characters.

Contrasting with the English settings and characters are the influences of the foreign experiences of the characters. The reader is informed that Watson has returned from Afghanistan wounded and without much money. Major Sholto and Captain Morstan both served abroad, but their lives have been negatively affected by their experiences. Most significantly, in Chapter 12, Jonathan Small is encouraged to tell his life story, most of which takes place in India. Small was originally a Worcestershire man from a family of farmers, but after getting **"into a mess over a girl"** joins the army and spends many years abroad *(Chapter 12)*. Although for other men this could have been a positive experience, he pays a steep price for his time abroad, losing a leg and then being arrested for theft and murder. His life in India is one of danger, punishment and violence, and it is fitting that he is finally captured in an English location described as being **'wild and desolate'** as was much of his life abroad *(Chapter 12)*.

Throughout the novel, there is a tension between the ideas of 'Englishness' and 'foreignness', and signs of both attraction and repulsion towards foreign influences. For example, Thaddeus Sholto's home could be seen as a symbolic representation of the uncomfortable combination of foreign and English tastes, as his exotic apartment is positioned bizarrely in a rundown English neighbourhood: **'There was something strangely incongruous in this Oriental figure framed in the commonplace doorway of a third-rate suburban dwelling-house'** *(Chapter 3)*. Thaddeus himself makes a very unlikely 'Sahib'. In addition, some critics feel that Chapter 12 sits uneasily within the novel as the action moves away from its London setting for such a long period and the adventures are so extreme and fast-paced, with Sherlock Holmes reduced to a supporting role.

Activity 4

Write a paragraph contrasting the depiction of Mrs Cecil Forrester's home with that of Thaddeus Sholto. Consider what attitudes Conan Doyle is displaying about each in his choice of their surroundings. Remember to choose precise phrases from the text to support your ideas.

Duality

Dual or split personality suggests strange undercurrents

Duality was a theme in many Victorian texts, in which a character may have a 'split personality' (as in *Strange Case of Dr Jekyll and Mr Hyde*, written by Robert Louis Stevenson in 1886) or assume false identities (such as those in Oscar Wilde's 1895 play, *The Importance of Being Earnest*). In Oscar Wilde's novel *The Picture of Dorian Gray*, which was commissioned for *Lippincott's Monthly Magazine* at the same time as *The Sign of Four*, an **amoral** man keeps his handsome and youthful appearance while there is a horrific, decaying portrait of him hidden away, which reveals his real nature. In *The Sign of Four* the reader is alerted to Holmes's darker side in the first chapter when he is scolded by Watson for indulging in drug use. In Chapter 7, Watson muses on how terrible it would be if Holmes's talents were used for crime rather than their detection and, in the novel's final chapter, Holmes quotes a German text that laments that he is only one man, when he could have been two: a good man and a rascal.

Other explorations of duality are evident in Holmes's pleasure in disguise. His ability to assume different personas, including that of an old sailor, seems to satisfy his need to explore different identities. His acquaintance with Mr McMurdo apparently stems from his willingness to assume the role of a boxer, without fear of personal injury.

Another example of duality is the role of the twins Thaddeus and Bartholomew Sholto, who could be viewed as a good twin and an evil twin. A particularly eerie effect is created when Thaddeus is standing beside Holmes and Watson, while they peer through a keyhole viewing his **doppelganger** – his dead brother.

In Victorian times there was an interest in contrasting acceptable society with its darker underside, and Conan Doyle's fascination with his changeable protagonist and the murkier side of human nature is evident in this novel.

amoral not based on moral standards, neither moral nor immoral
doppelganger a surprising double of a person

> **Key quotations**
>
> 'He was bright, eager, and in excellent spirits, a mood which in his case alternated with fits of the blackest depression.' *(Chapter 3)*
>
> "Strange," said I, "how terms of what in another man I should call laziness alternate with your fits of splendid energy and vigour."
> *(Chapter 12)*

> **Activity 5**
>
> With a partner, discuss why you think Conan Doyle chose to make Thaddeus and Bartholomew twins rather than simply brothers.

> **Tips for assessment**
>
> *Upgrade*
>
> When preparing to write about duality you should make notes about any times when characters are in disguise or appear to have two sides to their nature.

Emotion versus rationality

Throughout the novel, Conan Doyle explores aspects of philosophy, sometimes explicitly. For example, in Chapter 7 he discusses the writings of Jean Paul Richter, a German philosopher, with Watson. This is in keeping with Conan Doyle's own philosophical explorations, as he rejected the Catholic religion in which he was raised and eventually settled on **spiritualism**. Although Holmes is not making a similar journey, his and Watson's openness to new ideas and philosophies is apparent. In some sections of the novel, it is clear that Holmes is searching for the meaning of life and man's place in the world.

The conflict between **rationality** and emotion is a point of tension in the novel. Without Watson's more human and passionate responses, Holmes's intellect may be too cold and unappealing to the reader. In Watson's accounts of Sherlock Holmes's adventures, the reader must decide if they are, as Holmes says, tinged with 'romanticism' rather than the **'analytical reasoning from effects to causes'** that Holmes prizes *(Chapter 1)*.

In addition to Watson and Holmes, other characters display varying degrees of rationality and emotion. Athelney Jones, for example, who is described by Holmes as having **'occasional glimmerings of reason'**, employs his 'common-sense' and proudly works through his hypothesis of Thaddeus's guilt, declaring **'so much we know'** *(Chapter 6)*. However, in his eagerness to solve the case and gain acclaim, his thought processes are shown to be faulty, based largely on prejudice, due to Thaddeus being **'not attractive'** and having a house **'full of Indian curiosities'**

Holmes pursues rational explanation

(Chapter 6). Ironically, he calls Holmes 'Mr Theorist' and warns him that he may **'find it a harder matter than you think'** *(Chapter 6).* Jones is a character who believes he is rational, but is depicted by Conan Doyle as being highly influenced by his preconceptions and pride.

Mary Morstan is another character who embodies both rationality and emotion, for example, sensibly bringing the pearl-box addresses for Holmes's inspection, setting out her case clearly and then 'briskly' leaving them *(Chapter 2).* However, she frequently needs to master her emotions: **'I could see from Miss Morstan's manner that she was suffering from the same feeling'** *(Chapter 3).* In contrast, **'Holmes alone could rise superior to petty influences'** *(Chapter 3).* Notably, in Chapter 7, Miss Morstan can no longer control her emotions and bursts into a **'passion of weeping'** in contrast to the calm, supportive role she had previously played.

rationality basing one's beliefs on facts and logical reasoning

spiritualism the belief that the spirits of the dead can communicate with the living

Activity 6

First look at the quotations below and decide if they are examples of emotion or rationality. Then choose three to use in a **PEE** (Point, Evidence, Explanation) paragraph about emotion and rationality.

- "There are hardly any data," he remarked. *(Chapter 1)*
- '… with considerable bitterness in my heart.' *(Chapter 1)*
- "No, no: I never guess." *(Chapter 1)*
- "What a very attractive woman!" *(Chapter 2)*
- "A client is to me a mere unit, a factor in a problem." *(Chapter 2)*
- "How often have I said to you that when you have eliminated the impossible, whatever remains, *however improbable*, must be the truth?" *(Chapter 6)*
- 'My sympathies and my love went out to her, even as my hand had in the garden.' *(Chapter 7)*

PEE the process used to make a **P**oint, give a quotation as **E**vidence and **E**xplain the point

Activity 7

Create a role-play in which you and a partner play Holmes and Watson and discuss their different attitudes towards love and marriage. Keep in mind each character's approach to emotion and rationality.

Writing about themes

Upgrade

It is essential for you to be able to identify and discuss themes. In your exam you will need to show how Conan Doyle's use of language, structure and form contribute to his presentation of ideas and themes.

Some theme-based questions you may be asked include:

- Explore the importance of foreign adventures to the characters.

- Compare and contrast the presentations of friendship in the novel.

- Compare the attitudes of the characters to love and friendship.

- How does Conan Doyle present crimes and the victims of crime in the novel?

- How is the theme of money and social class presented in the novel?

- How is the character of Jonathan Small used to explore the theme of crime and justice in the novel?

- How is the relationship of Watson and Holmes used to explore the theme of friendship in the novel?

- How is the theme of duality presented in the novel?

- Explain why Conan Doyle's use of place and setting is important in the novel.

In order to prepare for theme-based questions you could:

- Choose and learn specific phrases to support your ideas about themes, such as those that demonstrate rationality or emotion.

- Make spider diagrams based on each of the main themes mentioned in this chapter and use these to make detailed notes in which you develop your arguments.

Exam skills

Understanding the question

Read the question carefully and underline the key words. Even if you think you have answered a similar question before, make sure you have identified exactly what is being asked of you in this particular question. Students often lose marks because they make basic errors such as answering only one part of a two-part question or writing about the wrong character or theme because they have misunderstood the main focus of the question.

Dealing with extracts in the exam

The point of giving you an extract in the exam is to invite a close reading of the text, which means picking out key words, phrases and literary devices, and analysing them with insight. This, in particular, is your opportunity to demonstrate your understanding of language, form and structure, as well as characterization and themes. The chosen extract will be rich in opportunities for locating key quotations and supporting your points. As you read the extract, annotate it, underlining key words or phrases that you may wish to quote and writing appropriate comments in the margins, such as 'simile' or 'surprising transition', to remind you to comment on these features. You will be asked to respond to the extract and make connections between your understanding of this extract and the rest of the novel.

Types and styles of questions

Here are some common types of questions with key words and phrases underlined, followed by an explanation of what each question requires.

Characters

How does the author present the character of Major Sholto in the novel?
'How' lets you know that you should be analysing rather than just describing the character. Wording such as 'the author present' or 'Conan Doyle present' reminds you to focus on the role of the author. The characters in the novel are not real people, but are constructed by Conan Doyle. While other characters appear in the novel and possibly within given extracts, the main focus of your response should be on the named character – Major Sholto in this case.

To what extent is Mary Morstan presented as a strong female character?
'To what extent' encourages you to create an argument in which you weigh up the evidence for or against a statement, although you may not entirely agree or disagree with it. You are explaining the degree to which you believe it is correct or not and supplying quotations to underpin your ideas. Your focus should be on the character of Mary Morstan, but your understanding of the restrictions on the lives of Victorian women and comparisons with the other female characters in the novel may be woven in to support your points about strong female characters.

Explore how the **attitudes and feelings** of **Dr Watson** are **portrayed** in the novel.

'Explore' suggests analysis rather than simply repeating what a character says, encouraging you to write in a more imaginative and insightful way. You may also wish to consider the differences between 'attitudes' and 'feelings'.

Themes

Explore how the **theme** of **crime** is **presented** in the novel.

The word 'explore' reminds you that you should analyse the literary techniques used to present crime rather than just listing the crimes that occur in the novel. Since a number of crimes are committed in the course of the novel, you will have to be selective and perhaps contrast the presentation of two or three crimes, leading to a point about the author's attitude towards each crime.

Relationships

Explore what we learn about the **relationship** between **Jonathan Small and Tonga**.

Relationship questions allow you to write about more than one character and to compare and contrast them. If this is a question relating to an extract printed in the exam paper, read through the extract carefully, looking for aspects of the relationship such as turning points, examples of affection or loyalty, and how positively the relationship is presented to the reader.

Setting

How does **Conan Doyle portray** the **setting** of **Pondicherry Lodge in this extract**?

'How' invites you to discover literary techniques such as alliteration or similes. You may consider how a certain mood or atmosphere is developed and how that contributes to the mystery.

Explore how the **author** uses **Victorian London** in this extract to create a **sense of mystery**.

This question encourages an imaginative exploration of the scene-setting in this chapter. As 'Victorian' is emphasized, an understanding of the context would support this answer, as well as the literary techniques used. Your points should lead to a greater understanding of how 'mystery' is created.

Language

How does the **author** use **language** to create **suspense** and **horror** in **this extract**?

Although any answer in an English Literature exam will deal with language in some way, this question reminds you to focus on this in detail. You will be expected to use correct literary terminology and analyse details from the extract. You may wish to consider how 'suspense' and 'horror' are different.

Planning your answer

Given the time pressure of exams, it is tempting to begin writing immediately. However, examiners point out that the best answers show clear evidence of planning. Planning is necessary to shape your response and to avoid basic errors, such as repetition or wandering off topic. However, planning needs to be sensible and time-efficient as well, so it is important that you discover the best method for you.

Below are some methods that you could use when approaching the following question:

Explore what we learn about the relationship between Jonathan Small and Tonga.

Spider diagrams

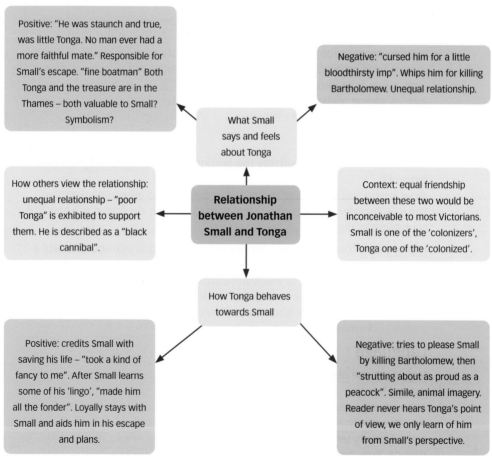

Positive: "He was staunch and true, was little Tonga. No man ever had a more faithful mate." Responsible for Small's escape. "fine boatman" Both Tonga and the treasure are in the Thames – both valuable to Small? Symbolism?

Negative: "cursed him for a little bloodthirsty imp". Whips him for killing Bartholomew. Unequal relationship.

What Small says and feels about Tonga

How others view the relationship: unequal relationship – "poor Tonga" is exhibited to support them. He is described as a "black cannibal".

Relationship between Jonathan Small and Tonga

Context: equal friendship between these two would be inconceivable to most Victorians. Small is one of the 'colonizers', Tonga one of the 'colonized'.

How Tonga behaves towards Small

Positive: credits Small with saving his life – "took a kind of fancy to me". After Small learns some of his 'lingo', "made him all the fonder". Loyally stays with Small and aids him in his escape and plans.

Negative: tries to please Small by killing Bartholomew, then "strutting about as proud as a peacock". Simile, animal imagery. Reader never hears Tonga's point of view, we only learn of him from Small's perspective.

Paragraphs

You may wish to begin by shaping your ideas into paragraphs; for example:

Paragraph 1: How unusual the relationship between Small and Tonga would have been in Victorian times (context). How Small's description of Tonga in Chapter 12 differs from previous images of him (structure/language).

Paragraph 2: Positive images of the relationship: 'staunch and true', mutual gratitude: Small heals Tonga and Tonga helps Small escape. Tonga is presented as the one loyal companion Small has found in his narrative (plot).

Paragraph 3: Unequal relationship: Tonga is 'exhibited' and 'whipped'. Animal imagery reinforces the earlier image of him being 'bestial' (language). Reader only learns about Tonga from the descriptions of others; he is allocated no dialogue so cannot give his own point of view (language/form/structure).

Paragraph 4: Symbolism: Small loses the things most valuable to him, the treasure and Tonga, to the Thames in the novel's resolution (language/structure).

Paragraph 5: Importance of this relationship in the narrative (form/structure) and what would have made this intriguing to Victorian readers (context).

Activity 1

Choose one of the sample questions from the beginning of this chapter and try creating both a spider diagram and a paragraph plan for it. Which method did you find most helpful and efficient?

Answering the question

It is important that you allow yourself a little thinking and planning time before answering your question so that you:

- structure your answer logically
- focus your answer correctly on all aspects of the question
- avoid missing out crucial points
- include a good range of quotations and literary terminology.

However, avoid spending too long writing up your plan. It should be in note form rather than long paragraphs of writing. Some students find a brief list is sufficient to help them put their ideas into a logical sequence and others just make a spider diagram surrounding the wording of the actual question. Don't spend more than a few minutes on the planning. Note your ideas and then begin.

In your first short introductory paragraph it is useful to employ some of the wording in the original question, as well as elsewhere in your essay, as this will ensure that you are staying on topic and answering the set question.

You should obviously be writing in a series of paragraphs and each of these should start with a **topic sentence**, which introduces the main point of that paragraph. You will then develop and support that idea with quotations from the text. In most cases, each of the central paragraphs of your essay should have several quotations from the text, followed by an explanation. You should end with a short conclusion, bringing together your ideas into a final point.

Tips for assessment

Upgrade

The most common error is for students simply to retell the plot or to describe a character or event. To avoid this, make sure that every paragraph includes ideas, evidence and analysis.

topic sentence the first sentence in a paragraph, which introduces the subject of main ideas that will follow

Timing

One of the most serious errors you can make in an exam is to get your timing wrong. If you need to answer more than one question in the exam, be aware of how many marks each question is worth and allocate your time appropriately. You may wish to plan this in advance. For example, if you have 1 hour and 45 minutes to answer two questions worth equal marks, you may wish to plan and write for 50 minutes on each question and then allow five minutes to check over your work for errors. English exams are designed to take the full time allocated, so if you finish early, you have probably not written enough.

Using quotations

You must support your ideas with evidence from the text. An extract-based question in the exam will help you with quotations for that extract. However, you will need to memorize some quotations from the text as a whole for non-extract-based questions. Once you have selected a quotation that helps you make your point, you should explain or analyse it. This process is often called PEE, which stands for Point, Evidence, Explanation. An example of this may be:

Point: Conan Doyle uses newspaper articles to highlight the irony of how Jones is perceived by the public.

Evidence: In Chapter 8, a newspaper article refers to Jones's 'trained and experienced faculties' that were directed to the 'detection of criminals' when the reader knows that Jones has clearly arrested the wrong man. The wording 'single vigorous and masterful mind' and 'well-known technical knowledge and his powers of minute observation' are ironic because they would better describe Holmes than Jones, who has leapt to entirely the wrong conclusions.

Explanation: Conan Doyle appears to be taking this opportunity to **satirize** the media, which has simply believed all of Jones's assertions without any supporting evidence and when he may be presenting himself in an overly confident way. This also highlights the contrast between Holmes, who appears to enjoy solving crimes as a private hobby, and Jones, who exploits the attention he receives to further his career. This is supported by Watson's comment at the end of the novel that Holmes has 'done all the work' and Jones 'gets the credit'. The humour of this situation is compounded when the second newspaper article has to announce the release of the wrongfully arrested Thaddeus and Mrs Bernstone, although they ironically remain convinced of Jones's unproven 'sagacity'.

satirize to mock or ridicule in order to point out aspects of vice, foolishness or weakness

Activity 2

1. Read the following student's answer about the importance of the relationship between Holmes and Watson. Then explain how it could have been improved by providing more evidence and explanation.

> The friendship between Holmes and Watson is very important in the novel. Watson admires Holmes and this is clear from many things he writes. He is also a retired army surgeon and sometimes yearns for the excitement of his past, which Holmes is able to provide. However, the two do not always see eye to eye on everything.

2. Choose one of the sample essay questions from this section and write your own Point, Evidence, Explanation (PEE) paragraph. Then try writing a chain of three different PEE responses on the same topic. See if you can link your paragraphs and avoid repetition.

Tips for assessment

When choosing quotations, it is best to select short excerpts of relevant words, phrases or sentences rather than copying out whole sections of the text. These should then be embedded into your writing in a grammatically correct way, as demonstrated in the PEE example on page 71.

Spelling, punctuation and grammar

Your spelling, punctuation and grammar (SPaG) is awarded marks in your exam. You will also make a much better impression on the examiner if your work is correctly written. Some writing errors are so severe that they can obscure your meaning, which will, of course, cost you marks. When you are practising timed writings, carefully check your work for errors. Common mistakes include:

- misspelling the title, author or names of the characters
- writing long, rambling, unshaped paragraphs
- forgetting to use common punctuation such as commas and apostrophes
- misusing capital letters
- writing 'texting' abbreviations such as 'u' for 'you'
- leaving out words
- lack of noun/verb agreement (such as 'he done' rather than 'he did').

In order to aim for more advanced and sophisticated writing, try:

- varying the opening of your sentences
- avoiding over-use of the word 'I'
- using linking phrases such as 'in contrast', 'ironically' or 'initially'
- employing phrases such as 'significantly' or 'most remarkably' to indicate when you are making your most important points.

Activity 3

With a partner, take it in turns to test each other on the spelling of all the main characters' names. Once you have mastered that, make a list of other tricky words and learn those as well.

Sample questions

1

Read the extract below and then answer both parts of the question.
Look at the extract in Chapter 1 from 'I sprang from my chair...' to "They are absolutely correct in every particular."
Beginning with the extract above, write about:
- how Conan Doyle portrays the relationship between Holmes and Watson in this extract
- how Conan Doyle portrays this relationship in the rest of the novel.

2

Use the extract below as a starting point to explore the role of women in the novel. Answer both parts of the question.
Look at the extract in Chapter 9 from 'I took our mongrel accordingly and left him...' to '... as though the matter was one in which she took small interest'.
- How does Conan Doyle portray the characters of Miss Morstan and Mrs Forrester in this extract?
- How does Conan Doyle portray the role of women in the rest of the novel?

3

Read the following extract and answer the question below.
Look at the extract in Chapter 4 from "When I first determined to make this communication to you..." to "I am partial to the modern French school."
How is the character of Thaddeus Sholto portrayed in this extract and the rest of the novel?

4

Read the extract below and answer the questions that follow.

Look at the extract in Chapter 10 from 'At that moment, however, as our evil fate would have it...' to '... as this mad, flying man-hunt down the Thames'.

Starting with the extract above, explore how Conan Doyle creates a sense of excitement and tension for the reader. Write about:

- how Conan Doyle creates excitement and tension in this extract
- how Conan Doyle creates tension elsewhere in the novel.

5

Read the following extract and answer the questions below.

Look at the extract in Chapter 7 from 'The police had brought a cab with them...' to 'This Agra treasure intervened like an impassable barrier between us.'

How is the theme of love presented in the novel? Starting with the extract above write about:

- the portrayal of love between Mary Morstan and Watson
- the portrayal of love in the rest of novel
- the social conventions and attitudes towards romance and marriage at this time.

6

Starting with the extract below, explore the importance of Pondicherry Lodge and other settings in adding to the mystery of the story.

Look at the extract in Chapter 5 from 'Inside, a gravel path wound through desolate grounds...' to '... the shrill, broken whimpering of a frightened woman'.

- How does Conan Doyle use the setting of Pondicherry Lodge in this extract to increase the sense of mystery and suspense?
- Explore other examples of settings in the novel contributing to the sense of mystery and suspense.

Sample answers

In this section you will see some sample questions and students' responses. These have been annotated with sample examiner comments to indicate where students may gain or lose marks.

Sample answer 1

> Referring first to the extract below and then to the rest of the novel, explain how Conan Doyle uses language to create suspense and horror in the novel.
>
> *Look at the extract in Chapter 5 from* "There is something devilish in this, Watson…" to "What is to be done?"

Appropriately uses some of the wording of the question.

Throughout the novel, Conan Doyle works at building up a sense of suspense, first when solving the mystery of the missing captain, but quickly escalating to the deaths of several characters.

Demonstrates understanding of the extract.

Chapter 5 contains one of the most chilling scenes in the novel. To build the suspense, Conan Doyle slowly leads the reader to the horrific discovery of Bartholomew Sholto's dead body.

One important means of emphasizing the suspense of the scene is its night-time setting. Conan Doyle emphasizes this by referring to 'Moonlight', 'moonlit room' and the 'shadow', which obscures everything but Bartholomew's face.

Embeds appropriate quotations.

Use of literary terminology.

The moon is personified as 'vague' and 'shifty', adding to its mysterious quality. To create horror, Conan Doyle uses the surprising adjective 'horrible' to describe the smile, followed by 'fixed' and 'unnatural', making the dead face seem even more grotesque. Adding to the horror of the scene is the dead man's identical resemblance to Thaddeus, who is standing beside them.

An interesting idea – could have introduced theme of duality.

This creates a certain supernatural eeriness as it appears as if Thaddeus is at once alive and dead. This ghost-like quality is further emphasized by the appearance that the face is 'suspended, as it were, in the air'. Though this is a trick of the shadows, it creates an alarming image.

This needs to be supported by evidence.

This is one of many deceptive images in the novel.

A clear topic sentence signalling a change in subject.

Watson's and Holmes' reactions to the scene also contribute to the reader's unease. Suspense is created by Holmes first taking in the scene without describing it and becoming more 'moved' than Watson has ever seen him before. As Holmes is famously calm and analytical, this show of emotion alerts the reader that something alarming is behind the door. Watson 'recoiled in horror' when he views the scene, further building suspense and anticipation in the reader. Watson is a former army soldier so would probably be used to seeing death, yet the macabre nature of this corpse particularly appals him.

Conan Doyle frequently uses night time and the unknown to increase the suspense in the novel. In Chapter 3, Watson, Holmes and Miss Morstan make a night-time journey, first to the Lyceum Theatre for an encounter with the mysterious letter writer. Watson describes the busy London scene as 'eerie and ghost-like' caused by the flickering light: 'they flitted from the gloom into light, and so back into the gloom once more'. As in Chapter 5, what is only partially seen is particularly unsettling. He also uses personification of the 'mud-coloured clouds', which 'drooped sadly'. The pathetic fallacy of this melancholy scene reflects Watson's mood as he is 'nervous and depressed', and Miss Morstan's is 'suffering from the same feeling'. Although nothing of particular importance has occurred in this section, Conan Doyle is preparing the reader for the enormity of later events.

Some well-chosen quotations.

Weak ending to paragraph – it should connect to question.

Significantly, the final chase also takes place at night in an exciting pursuit on the Thames. Some of the suspense is diminished by the title of Chapter 10 'The End of the Islander', which alerts the reader to Tonga's impending death. However, the eeriness and horror of his death is again emphasized by what is unseen. At first, Tonga is described as a 'dark mass' and 'like a Newfoundland dog'. This is one of several similes comparing Tonga to an animal and emphasizes what are perceived as his more bestial aspects. Like Bartholomew, only his face is 'exposed' and it is described in grotesque terms: 'deeply marked with all bestiality and cruelty'. However, he is only partly seen in the 'light of a lantern' so retains his mystery. Without ever being truly encountered but only 'glimpsed' by Holmes and Watson, he disappears amid the 'white swirl of the waters'. The image of his 'venomous, menacing eyes' as he goes to his death, as well as the near miss from the poisoned dart, add to the horror of this scene.

Shows understanding and uses of literary terminology.

Throughout the novel there is a conscious raising and releasing of tension. The novel was originally written for a magazine and Conan Doyle would have been aware of the need to keep the reader interested and intrigued. While happy to explore dangerous scenes and grotesque deaths, he often lightens the mood with comic relief or resolves the danger with an explanation.

Attempts to use context – a rushed conclusion.

This is a confident response demonstrating very good understanding of the novel. The candidate uses literary terminology well and stays generally focused on the question, although some sections are a little under-developed. A stronger conclusion would have gained it more marks.

Sample answer 2

Read the extract below and then discuss the presentation of women in both this extract and the novel as a whole.

> Look at the extract in Chapter 7 from 'It was nearly two o'clock when we reached Mrs Cecil Forrester's...' to '... in the midst of the wild, dark business which had absorbed us'.

A strong opening demonstrating contextual understanding.

Demonstrates understanding of whole novel.

In Victorian times, women were often idealized as 'the Angel in the House' and this description of the Forrester home supports this idea. This 'English home' is quite unlike the other settings in the novel, such as Holmes' Baker Street bachelor flat, Thaddeus Sholto's decadent apartment or the ominous and Gothic Pondicherry Lodge of Bartholomew Sholto, and it can be assumed that this is due to the 'graceful' presence of Mrs Forrester. The adverbs 'tenderly' and 'earnestly' are used to describe her actions and the effect of her home is 'soothing' and 'tranquil' in stark contrast to the more exciting and frightening adventures outside.

Clear topic sentence.

Mary Morstan is the most important female character in the novel and she is presented as being a bright and sympathetic character. Watson is immediately taken by her 'refined and sensitive nature' and Holmes declares her a 'model client'. Although she shows strength of character, she is also presented as being a highly feminine character, as would be acceptable to a Victorian reader. In this excerpt, she is 'graceful' and 'clinging', the second of these adjectives perhaps being less

Interesting idea but needs clearer explanation.

appealing to a modern reader, and in Chapter 2 'her lips trembled, her hand quivered', showing her as someone who has to work hard to overcome her 'inward agitation'. In Chapter 7, she is finally overcome by emotion. Watson refers to 'the angelic fashion of women' to remain calm when they have to support those weaker than themselves, which has resonances with the idea of 'the Angel in the House', but when relieved of looking after others, she 'burst into a passion of weeping'. Despite evidence of her strength, she is regarded as someone who must be looked after either by Watson who escorts her home or Mrs Forrester who meets her at the door.

Confident use of literary context.

In Victorian times there were limited job opportunities open to women and, like literary heroines before her such as Jane Eyre, Miss Morstan is a governess. However, the extract above makes it clear that she is 'no mere paid dependent' but an 'honoured friend'. In her current situation she has little opportunity for independence, but if she were to inherit the disputed treasure she would become an heiress and gain either financial independence or become a very desirable marriage proposition. This makes her reaction to the treasure, which she responds to 'coolly' and 'calmly' more admirable. Conan Doyle uses the metaphor of the 'treasure' to describe what Watson has gained in winning Mary's love. Although clearly meant to be positive, a modern reader may feel that this highlights Mary's lack of independence, that she will be someone else's possession.

Use of literary terminology.

Considers different readers' responses.

The female characters are not depicted as having the exciting adventures of the male characters. Mary is escorted away from danger and she must wait at home to learn the outcome of the race to capture the treasure, just as Mrs Forrester had to wait at home to discover the results of Mary's meeting with the mysterious letter writer. Other female characters like Mrs Hudson or Mrs Smith are mainly seen in domestic surroundings. Mrs Hudson, Mrs Smith and Mrs Forrester are depicted to some degree in taking a 'motherly' role, with Mrs Hudson fussing about Holmes' moods, Mrs Forrester showing concern for Mary and Mrs Smith chasing after her 'imp' of a son. These depictions are all quite sympathetic and fit with Dr Watson's positive opinion of women, contrasting with Holmes' more negative one. Conan Doyle seems to welcome the domesticating effect women can have upon men (there are no women presented in Jonathan Small's adventures) but they are restricted to a comforting and domestic role, to be kept separate from the 'dark business' that absorbs the men.

Another clear topic sentence, which is then well supported.

Sophisticated points but needs concluding paragraph.

This is quite a bold and lively response with a clear sense of developing an argument. She considers how different readers may respond to the female characters and demonstrates an understanding of the context. Some literary terminology is used, but the response would be improved by more language and structural analysis, such as discussing Watson's narrative voice.

Sample answer 3

Explore how Conan Doyle presents the theme of wealth in the novel.

Avoid starting your responses with 'I'.

The opening needs a more academic, analytical tone.

I think money has always been important and, in the novel, it is clear that many people are fighting over money. Captain Morstan dies because he goes to confront Major Sholto over money and Jonathan Small spends much of his life in prison because he wanted money. It has been said that 'Money is the root of all evil' and that could certainly be the case in this novel.

Shows some understanding but needs analysis.

The first time money is mentioned in the story is when Sherlock Holmes says that Watson's 'unhappy' brother, who drank too much, wasted his money and had to take his watch to the pawnshop. That this was considered shameful in Victorian times is clear from Watson's angry reaction. This shows the reader that money is important. We also know that Watson is ashamed to be a retired army surgeon on 'half-pay'.

Too much retelling of plot without analysis.

Wealth is also important because Mary Morstan has been receiving a mysterious gift of a valuable pearl every year. It turns out that she is owed a share of a treasure from the Sholtos, but the treasure disappears before she gets any. If she does get her share of the inheritance she will be an 'heiress' which is disappointing to Watson as he feels that then he cannot marry her.

Needs to focus more on the extract. Too informal.

Much of the plot revolves around attempts to recover the missing treasure. Some readers think that the treasure is cursed because it seems to bring bad luck to whoever owns it – it doesn't do anyone any good. Perhaps it is for the best that it ends up at the bottom of the Thames.

Misses the opportunity to discuss language here.

I believe the message of the novel is not to obsess about wealth or treasures because nothing good seems to come out of it. Watson is happy that the treasure is lost as he thinks Mary Morstan will now become his 'treasure'.

Correct use of literary terminology.

One example of wealth in the novel is Thaddeus Sholto's apartment. It is described as looking 'as out of place as a diamond of the first water in a setting of brass'. This simile shows the apartment looks rich and opulent but is placed in a very common, ordinary house. Thaddeus Sholto is one of the characters who does seem to enjoy his wealth as he considers himself a 'patron of the arts' and he is surrounded by objects which he finds beautiful. But the reader may wonder about how admirable or happy his lifestyle is, as he seems to live a rather lonely and isolated life.

Wealth has had an even more negative impact on his brother Bartholomew, who loses his life shortly after discovering the treasure he has spent many years searching for. Even his own home has been destroyed, as it is described as looking 'as though all the moles in England had been let loose'. This simile makes it sound almost funny that the grounds of what was probably a very grand house have been ruined and shows the desperation of Bartholomew to gain the treasure. Ultimately, Bartholomew pays with his life, as once he discovers the treasure, he is killed by Small.

A more promising paragraph.

Major Sholto also pays a big price for his desire for treasure. When he is a soldier he gambles away much of his money and is facing disgrace. He then decides to steal the treasure from Small by betraying him and the rest of the 'Four'. However, when he is at home he seems haunted by the fear that Small will seek revenge and he dies an unhappy man. Also his fight with Captain Morstan over the treasure costs him a friendship.

Under-developed ideas – needs to discuss theme.

In the end, the treasure ends up at the bottom of the Thames and maybe that is the best place for it!

A very informal ending without reference to the original question.

This is an example of a response that needed better planning and more focus on the extract. The candidate has a good understanding of the plot of the novel, but never mentions the word 'theme' and doesn't analyse language, form or structure. To gain more marks, a better selection of quotations, more analysis of the extract and less retelling of plot were needed. Occasionally the tone is too informal.

Sample answer 4

> Read the extract below from *The Sign of Four* and then answer the two questions below.
>
> *Look at the extract in Chapter 6 from 'He whipped out his lens and a tape measure...' to '"Why, we have got him, that's all," said he.'*
>
> Explore how Conan Doyle presents Sherlock Holmes as a fascinating character:
> - in this extract
> - in the novel as a whole.

Confident opening and immediate use of terminology. →

Through the admiring narration of Dr Watson, Conan Doyle presents Sherlock Holmes as a fascinating character, whose extremes in energy and lethargy, and capacity for good and evil, make him a surprising and exciting protagonist. The reader, like Watson, is always two steps behind Holmes, and is put in the position of observing him with wonder and puzzlement.

Impressive close reading of text. →

Considers effects of the author's choices. →

In this extract, the reader is presented with Holmes at his energetic best. Using animal similes, Watson compares him to birds and a trained bloodhound as he eagerly pursues the clues to Bartholomew Sholto's murder. His sharp eyes are 'like those of a bird' and he can pick up a scent with furtive movements 'like those of a trained bloodhound'. This presents him as having almost super-human capabilities in crime detection. The list of verbs 'measuring, comparing, examining' emphasizes his energetic action, making it seem as if he is doing this at an almost impossible pace, without pausing for thought. He also seems entirely uninhibited when seeking his criminal as he is said to be 'muttering to himself' and like a large bird 'broke into a loud crow of delight'. This moment of discovery surprises the reader by its suddenness and also creates mystery as the reader does not yet know what Holmes has discovered.

Clear topic sentence. →

Considers sophisticated theme. →

However, in addition to this discussion of Holmes's detection techniques, is Watson's meditation on Holmes' potential for evil as well as good. He remarks that he could not think 'what a terrible criminal he would have made had he turned his energy and sagacity against the law'. This duality in Holmes is commented on in several sections of the novel. When the reader is first introduced to him, he is injecting himself with cocaine, which while not illegal in Victorian times, was not really approved of either, as is clear from Watson's reaction. It would seem that when Holmes is bored he can get up to mischief, so it is very lucky that a criminal case comes to occupy him. Duality was an important theme in Victorian literature, such as in novels like 'Dr Jekyll and Mr Hyde', and the Victorian reader may have been curious to see if Holmes would ever tip over into his 'dark' side. Holmes refers explicitly to this duality at the end of the novel when he quotes Xenian (a German text), in which he bemoans that he is both a good man and a rascal.

Understands literary context.

In Chapter 7, the reader gains insight into the more philosophical side of Holmes when he reacts to the beauty of the morning and compares the 'great elemental forces' with 'our petty ambitions and strivings'. This is a surprising conversation for the detective to be having (especially while being led by a sniffer dog in pursuit of a criminal) and this is the sort of intriguing detail that Conan Doyle has included to increase the fascination with Holmes. He can change moods immediately and ends his philosophical meditation by asking Watson if he has a pistol. He goes immediately from being a man of thought to a man of action.

Effectively returns to the idea of fascination.

Needs more development of this idea.

Conan Doyle also presents Sherlock Holmes as a difficult friend to Watson. On one hand, there is a great deal of respect, but Holmes can neglect Watson's feelings. In the first chapter he is shown forgetting how 'personal and painful' memories of Watson's brother might be and in the last chapter reacts rudely and bluntly to Watson's engagement: 'I really cannot congratulate you.' The reader, and Watson (who in both cases is hurt), cannot anticipate Holmes' reactions and that remains one of the sources of his fascination.

Could tie in more clearly to question.

The novel returns full circle to Holmes once again reaching for his 'seven per cent solution' in order to relieve himself of his boredom. Instead of the joyous Holmes seen pursuing the criminal, a certain melancholy steals over him, only to be relieved by his next case.

Comments on the structure of the novel.

This candidate deftly explores some sophisticated ideas such as duality and frequently analyses the effect of the author's choices. A very sound understanding of the whole novel is demonstrated as well as some confident use of literary terminology. A few points could be developed by relating more clearly to the idea of 'fascination' and it needs a clearer conclusion.

Glossary

acumen cleverness or insight

Aesthetic Movement an arts movement in the latter half of the 19th century, which promoted 'art for art's sake'. Followers favoured highly decorative objects and were often influenced by exotic artefacts being brought into Europe at the time

affectation speech or behaviour that appears artificial, attention-seeking or designed to impress others

alliteration the use of the same first letter or sound in words that are next to one another or very closely grouped together

amoral not based on moral standards, neither moral nor immoral

anthropomorphism attributing human characteristics to an animal or object

atmosphere the mood or tone established in the writing

automaton a mechanical device that appears to be human

avarice extreme greed or desire for wealth

catalyst something that causes an event

chase sequence an exciting, action-packed hunt for a person or object, often in films

chronological arranged in the order of time in which events occurred

climax the most exciting and tense section of the novel, which usually occurs near the end

clue evidence used for the detection of crime

colonialism the settling, transformation and restructuring of new territories

comic relief amusing or light-hearted episodes that provide a break or contrast from more serious aspects

complication a plot or character detail that increases interest and is not easily resolved

conundrum a difficult riddle or puzzle

decorum proper, dignified and socially acceptable behaviour

denouement the final part of a novel when the various strands of the plot are brought together and resolved; also called the resolution

dialect particular pronunciations and word choices used by people of a particular geographical region

dialogue the speeches or conversations in a book or play

diction choice of words

doppelganger a surprising double of a person

duality made up of two opposing parts, such as good and evil

empathy understanding and identification with the feelings, thoughts or actions of another

enigma something that is very puzzling and hard to understand

exposition description and explanation of ideas; usually used in the first part of a novel when characters and themes are introduced, but also used elsewhere, for example to give background information

first-person narrator a narrator who is usually one of the characters in the novel and writes about events from a single perspective, using the word 'I'

flashback a narrative device in which the chronological order of the story is interrupted and events from an earlier time are presented

forensics crime scene forensics involves the gathering of evidence, which can lead to the courtroom conviction of a criminal

foreshadowing a literary device in which the author hints at what will happen at a later point

hieroglyphic writing that resembles Ancient Egyptian scripts, which used pictures and symbols

hypochondriac a person with exaggerated worries about his or her health

imagery the use of visual or other vivid language to convey ideas or emotions

imperialism the claiming and exploiting of new territories

intuition arriving at a truth or solution without relying on reasoning; a quick insight

irony words that express the opposite of what is meant; the difference between what may be expected and what actually occurs; it can also be used to make the reader or audience aware of something unknown to the characters (dramatic irony)

'locked room' murder a seemingly impossible murder, where, due to a door being locked from the inside, it is difficult to see how the murderer would have escaped

malevolence the state of wishing ill on others or having evil intentions

melodramatic having the features of a melodrama, a popular type of play in Victorian times, typically containing extreme characters, exaggerated emotions and sentimental themes

metaphor a comparison of one thing to another to make a description more vivid; unlike a simile, it does not use the words 'like' or 'as', but states that something is something else

narrator a person who tells a story

omniscient narrator an all-knowing narrator who can relate the thoughts and feelings of many characters, usually written in the third person

paradox an apparently contradictory statement or situation, such as Watson wanting to find the treasure and also hoping that he doesn't

pathetic fallacy the assigning of human emotions to aspects of nature, such as 'laughing sunlight' or 'cruel rain'

PEE the process used to make a **P**oint, give a quotation as **E**vidence and **E**xplain the point

personification when human qualities are given to something non-human, such as an object or idea

philosophy a set of beliefs or values that underpin the way one chooses to live one's life and understand the surrounding world

post-colonial criticism a type of literary criticism, which focuses both on texts by writers from nations, such as Britain, that colonized others, and on texts by writers from nations, such as India, that were colonized. It often questions the perspectives of the colonizers and seeks to discover alternative points of views. It explores concepts such as power, politics, religion and culture

pragmatism having a sensible and realistic attitude, with an understanding of what is possible and achievable

preternatural exceptional, abnormal or supernatural

protagonist the central character in the novel

proxy a person who represents someone else

rationality basing one's beliefs on facts and logical reasoning

Realism a literary movement that began in the mid-19th century and encouraged looking at the world as it really is rather than in a more romantic, implausible way. Realist authors often focused more on middle- and working-class characters and recounted the details of their everyday lives. Although Conan Doyle is not a typical realist author, aspects of this movement can be found in his work

red herring a clue that misleads the reader and encourages a false conclusion

sarcasm a type of irony, using words to mean the opposite of what is said, often creating either a comic or insulting effect

satirize to mock or ridicule in order to point out aspects of vice, foolishness or weakness

simile a comparison of one thing to another, using 'like' or 'as'

sociolect particular pronunciations and word choices used by people of a particular social class

spiritualism the belief that the spirits of the dead can communicate with the living

street Arabs homeless children or urchins; this term, rarely used now, is sometimes seen as offensive as it refers to the nomadic life of Arabs

sub-plot a second plot, which runs alongside the main plot

syntax the structure of sentences, including word order and grammar

theme a topic or idea that appears in literature

third-person narrator the form used by omniscient narrators, which uses 'he' or 'she' rather than 'I'

topic sentence the first sentence in a paragraph, which introduces the subject of main ideas that will follow

OXFORD
UNIVERSITY PRESS

Great Clarendon Street, Oxford OX2 6DP United Kingdom

Oxford University Press is a department of the University of Oxford. It furthers the University's objective of excellence in research, scholarship, and education by publishing worldwide. Oxford is a registered trade mark of Oxford University Press in the UK and in certain other countries

British Library Cataloguing in Publication Data

Data available

ISBN 978-0-19-835530-4
Kindle edition ISBN 978-0-19-836899-1

10 9 8 7 6 5 4

Printed in Hong Kong by Sheck Wah Tong

Acknowledgements

Cover: © Q44/Alamy, ostill/Shutterstock; **p1:** © Q44/Alamy, ostill/ Shutterstock; **p8:** REX/Alex Milan Tracy; **p18:** Efired/Shutterstock; **p21:** © Pictorial Press Ltd/Alamy; **p22:** © AF archive/Alamy; **p26:** © GL Archive/Alamy; **p28:** © Mary Evans Picture Library/Alamy; **p34:** © Photos 12/Alamy; **p36:** © AF archive/Alamy; **p42:** Joan Wakeham/REX; **p50:** © Bon Appetit/Alamy; **p53:** © AF archive/Alamy; **p55:** © Pictorial Press Ltd/Alamy; **p59:** © AF archive/Alamy; **p61:** Sabine Scheckel/Getty Images; **p63:** © lorenzo rossi/Alamy; **p65:** © Moviestore collection Ltd/ Alamy

Artwork courtesy of Simon Tegg.

Extracts are taken from *Arthur Conan Doyle: Sherlock Homes: Selected Stories* edited by Barry McCrea (Oxford World Classics, 2014).